Explore the Old City of Aleppo

Come with Tamim to a World Heritage Site

Khaldoun Fansa

Illustrated by Abdalla Asaad
Translated by Mustafa Merza and Munzer Absi
Edited by Mamoun Sakkal, PhD, and John D. Berry

 Cune

"To the origin; to the original and the noble; to the spirit of my mother. To my family: my wife and my children."

—*Khaldoun Fansa*

Explore the Old City of Aleppo: Come with Tamim to a World Heritage Site by Khaldoun Fansa © 2020 Khaldoun Fansa
Hardback ISBN 9781951082154 $24.00
Illustrator: Abdalla Assad. Translators: Mustafa Merza; Munzer Absi. Editors: Mamoun Sakkal, PhD; John D. Berry. Graphic Design: Mamoun Sakkal. Cune Press, Seattle 2020 [previously published in paperback under the title *Visit the Old City of Aleppo*]

Library of Congress Cataloging-in-Publication Data

Names: Fansa, Khaldoun, author. | Assad, Abdalla, illustrator. | Merza, Mustafa, translator. | Absi, Munzer A., translator.
Title: Explore the old city of Aleppo : come with Tamim to a World Heritage Site / Khaldoun Fansa ; illustrated by Abdalla Asaad.
Other titles: Visit the old city of Aleppo
Description: First edition. | Seattle : Cune Press, 2020. | Previously issued by publisher as: Visit the old city of Aleppo.

Identifiers: LCCN 2019035059 | ISBN 9781951082154 (hardback) | ISBN 9781614573357 (kindle edition) | ISBN 9781614573364 (ebook) Subjects: LCSH: World Heritage areas--Syria--Aleppo--Juvenile literature. | Aleppo (Syria)--Description and travel--Juvenile literature. | Aleppo (Syria)--History--Juvenile literature. | Aleppo (Syria)--Pictorial works. Classification: LCC DS99.A56 F36 2020 | DDC 956.91/3--dc23 LC record available at https://lccn.loc.gov/2019035059

Summary: "Khaldoun Fansa is an Aleppo native who was displaced by the Syrian Civil War. For many years he worked as an architect who managed restoration of Aleppo's Old City for private owners as well acting as a consultant for the Aga Khan Trust. Exploring the Old City of Aleppo is Fansa's effort to keep Syrian culture alive in a difficult time and to prepare for the day when the cannons are silent and women and men of good will can begin to rebuild their city and their lives. Exploring the Old City of Aleppo is a book for children as well as a book for adults who may choose to read aloud to a child. The narrative follows young Tamim and his father on their explorations of the Old City, pre civil war. Accent pages provide insights from 5,000 years of culture and history reflected in the houses, covered markets, and narrow alleyways. Aleppo was a major trading center built of Roman stone that continued to flourish in the time of Marco Polo and later served as the favored British trading route to India. Aleppo's Old city is listed as a UNESCO world heritage site"-- Provided by publisher.

Explore the Old City of Aleppo (hardcover) and Visit the Old City of Aleppo (paperback) were awarded the Alassadi Heritage Award for 2019 by the Friends of Al-Adeyat Archaeological Society, Montreal, presented by Dr. Nahed Koussa under the patronage of Al-Adeyat Archaeological Society, Aleppo, Syria.

Syria Crossroads (a series from Cune Press)

Stories My Father Told Me	Helen Zughaib, Elia Zughaib
Leaving Syria	Bill Dienst & Madi Williamson
The Plain of Dead Cities	Bruce McLaren
Steel & Silk	Sami Moubayed
Syria - A Decade of Lost Chances	Carsten Wieland
The Road from Damascus	Scott C. Davis
A Pen of Damascus Steel	Ali Ferzat
White Carnations	Musa Rahum Abbas
The Dusk Visitor	Musa Al-Halool

Cune www.cunepress.com

Contents

From the Author

- **For whom is this Book intended?**
- How can Syrians secure a place among civilized societies if we are not fully aware of our own heritage?
- Is the tyranny of modernity going to make us forget the history and geography of our region?
- How can we preserve our identity and origins in this age? And how can we face globalization at a time when it imposes its hegemony on the world as a whole?

Such questions drove me to create Visit the Old City of Aleppo.

In the current day, many of Syria's heritage treasures have been buried under ill-considered construction or looted by thieves with backhoes, or blasted to pieces by malicious military commanders. Much has been destroyed—collateral damage—in the jousting of armies and militias.

The Old City of Aleppo is a vessel that holds knowledge of our architecture and building sciences. It is a reference for our fine arts as well as our crafts, an authentic document of our human experiences, all in one location.

Across the world, the conservators of traditional cultures worry that the young will be socialized to an emerging, electronic, youth culture of undeniable appeal that, in the long term, is shallow, uprooted, and lacking in spiritual sustenance.

Visit the Old City of Aleppo is addressed to the young as well as the old. It tells the story of ancient Aleppo: its origins, its history, its people—those who lived here in the past and those who live here today.

This book is an effort to transmit our history and heritage to our young ones.

We owe this to Aleppo, the city that nurtured us in the past and now, as reconciliation and rebuilding begin, will provide a touchstone for the renewal of our civilization.

—Khaldoun Fansa

Symbols used in the dialogue sections

 Tamim

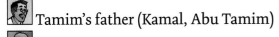 Tamim's father (Kamal, Abu Tamim)

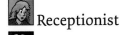 Receptionist

 Fadi

 Fadi's father (Dr. Wadie, Abu Fadi)

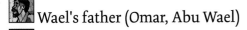 Fadi's Grandmother

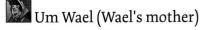 Wael's father (Omar, Abu Wael)

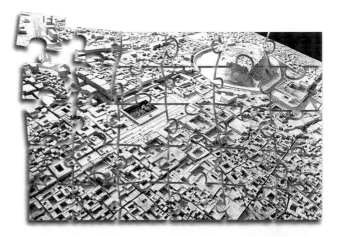 Um Wael (Wael's mother)

To the Reader

The layout and editing of this book was based on the interaction between two sections, first the *Tale* and second the *Facts*. They are woven together throughout the book, since they relate to each topic in the book.

The simple tale of this book appears in the form of dialogue between a father and his son during selected tours they made to some locations in the Old City of Aleppo. The tale was enriched with illustrations and pictures that expressed different scenarios and situations.

Moreover, some supporting texts were used to give a synopsis of facts about certain locations in Old Aleppo, and identified by this scroll background.

The tale, illustrations, pictures, and factual texts form together a puzzle that illustrate and illuminate the features of Old Aleppo. Each of them is a piece that helps complete the portrait. A reader may not find the portrait completely rendered by the end of the book. This will be an incentive for him or her to complete this portrait. After reading, he or she may visit other areas and locations to discover other things not mentioned in the pages of this book, so that he or she can obtain knowledge and enjoyment at the same time.

طـ Aleppo

1

The Beginning

Tamim was a twelve-year old boy whose father's name was Kamal. Tamim was a curious child, alert, and quick-minded. In school, he was a high achiever. One Saturday morning, he walked into his father's office and saw him sitting at his desk reviewing several books that lay open and papers that were scattered about. On one side of the desk was his father's computer with a monitor and a keyboard. In the background was calm and soothing music, giving the room an air of peacefulness and tranquility. The music playing was a tune by Mozart, one of his father's favorite composers.

Tamim was holding a large piece of paper with colored drawings on it.

Dad! Take a look at what I drew.

What's that? A landscape drawing! How beautiful! When did you draw it?

I started drawing it about an hour ago.

Where did you come up with this scene?

Out of my own mind.

You mean out of your memory.

Yes, Dad. I came up with it having seen lots of scenes that I liked and remembered, and I drew this one.

Well done, Tamim. But I advise you to draw nature as you see it. Train your eyes to stay focused on the scene while your hand immediately draws what you see.

But that would mean going out a lot to look at nature in order to draw it. I may not be able to do that very often unless we go on a picnic together or if I go on a trip with my class at school.

That's right. Next time when we go on a picnic, don't forget to take your crayons and papers. But tell me Tamim, do you like drawing?

Yes, Dad. I love to draw.

That means you can draw anything you see: this table, the vase on it, that chair, that fruit bowl over there, and just about anything you see in the street. You can draw cars and trees. You can draw nature when you see it and as you see it. This gives your eyes the ability to pay attention to detail and makes your hand flexible in drawing what you see.

Thanks, Dad.

Tamim noticed a picture among his father's papers. It looked like an aerial view of a city with an oval-shaped structure in the center. He asked his father:

What's that in the picture, Dad? Is it a city?

Tamim's father was busy writing, so he answered his son with a question.

What city, Tamim?

That … in that picture. Isn't it a city? With its buildings as seen from the top? And what's that oval shape in the center of the picture?

Oh! This is Aleppo. You don't recognize it? You were born here. Maybe you're right, you don't know old Aleppo.

I was born in Aleppo and have lived in it all my life, yet I don't know old Aleppo. I don't know these buildings, and I've never seen the Citadel.

Aerial view of old city of Aleppo with Citadel

Kamal put down his pen and looked at his son:

You are still young, Tamim. You have plenty of time to visit the old city of Aleppo. People come from all over the world to see it.

But I've never visited the old city, Dad.

You live in modern Aleppo, surrounding the old city, so it is natural that you don't know much about its older section. Yes, Tamim, old Aleppo is the very heart of the city, like the heart of one's body.

Dad, are you saying that the city, like the body, has a head, a heart, arms, and legs?

Tamim's father took a folded paper and opened it. It was a map of Aleppo.

Yes, Tamim, the city is like a human being. It goes through birth, growth, and aging just like a human body does. That's because people live and move in it. It is made up of people who affect it and get affected by it.

He passed his right hand over the map and continued his explanation:

This is the Citadel of Aleppo, and that's its heart.

Tamim's eyes sparkled with enthusiasm and curiosity.

Dad . . . tell me more about Aleppo. How was it started? How did it grow? Who called it Aleppo and why?

Tamim's father folded the papers that were between his hands, looked Tamim in the eye, and responded:

You've got so many questions. It's best for us to visit Old Aleppo and see it together. There, the answers will be more clear and they will stick deep into your memory.

A Historical Survey of Aleppo

The name Aleppo was reportedly first mentioned in the tablets found in the Ebla archives at Tal Mardikh (southwest of Aleppo) dating back to the third millennium BC.

Texts discovered in the city of Mari dating back to the second millennium BC (where excavations under Tal al-Hariri in the Syrian Jazeera took place) prove that the prosperous Kingdom of Yamhad had a capital city called Hal Ba. The Hittites (1700 BC) called it Halba.

During the classic period (312 BC–636 CE(the city was named Beroea. Later, Arabs restored its old name, calling it Halab. Italian traders pronounced this name "Aleppo," and this name has been used among non-Arabic speakers ever since.

Archaeological excavations in the layers underneath the Citadel's surface in 1929 uncovered a basalt relief stone measuring about four feet by three feet, which caught the attention of archaeologists. Why it was there? They later asserted that the stone dated back to the Hittite period in Syria. It was then preserved in the Aleppo Museum and is currently on display in the museum's courtyard.

After much research and investigation, the

Aerial view of Citadel and its environs

Basalt relief discovered in Citadel

University of Berlin offered to carry out excavations in the Citadel. A joint German-Syrian mission was formed for that purpose, and work started in 1996. The mission uncovered a Hittite temple about four thousand years old, from the beginning of the 2nd millennium BC (the Middle Bronze Age).

View of Storm God Temple area before excavations, 1983

View of Storm God Temple excavations, 2003

The mission thus provided a clue to one of the mysteries in Syria's ancient history, for it revealed that the site was one of the world's most ancient sites of human habitation. The Aleppo Citadel was first built as a sacred temple, but later transformed into a residential settlement. As time passed, the construction around the Citadel was extended, with other waves of construction to the south.

It is now believed that Aleppo had been settled as far back as the 6th and 5th millennia BC, when humans in the New Stone Age settled on a hill that was 130 feet higher than the surrounding area and located near the Quwaqe River.

Aleppo has seen prosperity since ancient times. Owing to its location south of the mountainous barrier of Anatolia, close by the Mediterranean, and near the Euphrates River, which flows to the Persian Gulf, Aleppo became a trading city. Merchants from all over the world converged on Aleppo, buying and selling metals, spices, jewels, timber, wheat, olive oil, and more.

Tamim smiled and said:

 Dad, I am with you. When are we going? Tomorrow? Great! But first, tell me more.

Well Tamim . . . what can I say? Sit down and listen. Some old texts say that Aleppo was born about five thousand years ago. Originally, construction started on a rocky hill that the first people found in this area. Over time, it became a habitation site for them and their holy temple. Then it turned into a defensive fort, which is the Citadel. Habitation went beyond the perimeter of the Citadel, forming a small town, which grew into a city with a Citadel at its core.

After that, the Citadel became a residence and a fortress for kings ruling the city. The walls constructed with large stones were built around the city. These walls had gates and defensive towers to repel invasions and attacks against it.

Tamim was eagerly listening to his father's explanations. He said in astonishment:

You mean to say Aleppo has been in existence for five thousand years! Oh my God, what an old place!

There is evidence that it is even older than that. Archaeologists found some ancient man-made pieces and tools in it going back to times before it became a city. It is the oldest continuously inhabited city in the world.

Why is it called Aleppo?

A smart question, Tamim. Back in olden times, people of the area—I mean Syria, which we live in now—didn't speak the Arabic we use today, but they spoke and wrote using ancient languages such as Canaanite, then Aramaic, then...

There was a moment of silence in which Tamim seemed confused and distracted.

Illustration of Citadel and old City from Bab Qinnisreen direction

Satellite view of old city of Aleppo, 1994

Aerial view of Citadel and old City

Tell me, Tamim, are you bored?

Tamim blinked his eyes as if he'd just gotten up from a nap. He said,

No, Dad, I hear you and I'm thinking about what you've said. But tell me, how did you collect all these pictures? How many albums have you got?

I started collecting them when I fell in love with the old city of Aleppo. That was a little over twenty-five years ago. Now I've got an assorted collection of photographs. Some of them are black-and-white, taken over a hundred years ago, when photography was first introduced into Syria. Then there are other photos that I took with my own camera. I also acquired photos from friends or from special publications about old Aleppo.

Did you start the hobby of taking pictures because of your love of old Aleppo?

Not exactly. As I'm an architect, I had an urge to photograph buildings or sites in old Aleppo in order to document and preserve some of their details in memory—beautiful details with magnificent ornamentation skillfully and meticulously crafted, revealing exceptional craftsmanship. I was worried that they would start to disappear.

A City with a Unique Character

Aleppo has assimilated artistic and cultural currents coming from all directions. Its people welcomed them, interacted with them, and shaped them through their own spirit into artistic forms. The result was outstanding monuments, superbly built and designed. Over time, Aleppo became the focus of many researchers and artists, who wrote about and depicted it in their art, thus providing valuable authentic documentation of the city's history.

Some may describe Old Aleppo as a large museum containing ancient monuments and historic buildings, a conservatory, so to speak, of diverse cultural creative works that make it appealing to those interested in archaeology.

Old Aleppo is also a place where people live and work. Aleppo is a thriving life form, rather than a museum or a dead city. Such was the birth of a project for the rehabilitation of the Old City of Aleppo.

The Organization of the Islamic Conference selected Aleppo as a Capital of Islamic Culture for 2006. This selection was based on a number of criteria such as:

–The urban heritage of Aleppo and its Islamic architecture serving various functions.

–Its rich cultural, scientific, and artistic assets and products.

–The effective economic role it has played since its inception and early life.

–Its location as one of the most important commercial meeting points on the Silk Road.

Aleppo is a trading city that has been characterized for generations by its religious tolerance, and the acceptance of others who are different. This has always made it possible for diverse religions, races, and denominations to live side-by-side. The city managed to assimilate previous cultures and civilizations. It displayed an elasticity of thought that enabled it to adapt and prosper as times changed. In Aleppo people were curious about strangers and expected to learn from them. Aleppo's way of life rested on the trader's insight that people from foreign lands bring wisdom and wealth.

Bab Qinnisreen neighborhood from minaret of Rumi mosque

Dad, aside from photos, how do you know all this information?

I love doing research and collecting information about the old city of Aleppo. Many people fell in love with this city before I did. They wrote about it, drew it, or took photographs. Some were historians, others were travelers. Some were Arabs, others were foreigners. So much has been written about Aleppo that it could fill the shelves of a large library. Many of these books, articles, and studies have yet to be translated into Arabic.

I heard a little about the old city of Aleppo, Dad. Our teacher at school promised to take us to the Citadel last spring, but it rained heavily on that day, so the trip was postponed. The kids from the next class who visited the Citadel told us about it. They said they found nothing interesting there, only old things, scattered stones. The teacher didn't explain what they saw, so the trip turned into a picnic where children played around and had a lot of fun but really didn't learn anything.

Let's see what you can learn, Tamim. I told you that the Citadel was the birthplace of the city of Aleppo, but I would like to add now that a wall-relief engraved upon a piece of black basalt stone was found in 1929 inside the debris of soil on the surface of the citadel. This discovery prompted excavations in the deep layers of the Citadel in order to find clues about the history of the Citadel and the city itself.

What was this relief? What was the reason for these excavations?

Tamim's father pulled a picture out of his collection and said:

Look at this picture… this relief stone inscription is now in the Museum of Aleppo.

When do we go to the Museum of Aleppo? When do we go to the Citadel?

Soon. Maybe the day after tomorrow. We'll start by seeing the citadel. That's enough for one day. What do you say?

Why not tomorrow?

Aerial view of Great Mosque and Citadel

Well, first of all, I'm busy tomorrow. I have a meeting and I need to run some errands. Anyway, the Citadel, the Museum, and all historical tourist attractions close on Tuesdays. It's their day-off.

OK. And I just remembered. The day after tomorrow is a holiday at school too. But what time can we go to the old city, Dad?

We need to start early. It's hard to find parking and there is a lot to see. We'll head for the Citadel and, on the way, we'll walk through the ancient alleyways and see some of the old houses.

I'm ready. *Yala, yala* Dad. Let's go!

Photograph of Bab Qinnisreen taken circa 1916

Photograph of Bab Qinnisreen taken circa 1916

Walls and Gates of the City

Populated cities in ancient times were fortified against enemy incursions. Thus the people of Aleppo erected walls around their city. As the city grew and evolved, it got larger and, during the Ayyubid period, outgrew its walls. Today residents refer to Old Aleppo as "Inside the Walls."

Gates were distributed around the walls where people entered and exited the city under the watchful eyes of guards. These gates were made of thick planking with iron hinges and metal cladding. When the doors were closed, they were nearly as impregnable as the stone walls of the Citadel, providing a state of the art defense against marauders and invading armies.

Aleppo had nine gates: Bab al-Faraj (previously known as Bab al-Faradis), Bab al-Nasr, Bab al-Hadid (previously known as Bab al-Qanat), Bab al-Ahmar, Bab al-Nairab, Bab al-Maqam (previously known as Bab al-Iraq), Bab Qinnisrien (which leads to the now dead town of Qinnisrien), Bab Antakiya (which leads to the seaport city of Antioch), and Bab al-Jinan. Four of Aleppo's gates have now vanished: Bab al-Faraj, Bab al-Ahmar, Bab al-Nairab, and Bab al-Jinan. Likewise, the wall around the city slowly fell into disrepair, after losing its defensive role with the invention of gun powder and cannons. Old Aleppo grew beyond its walls, and suburbs were

Photograph of Bab al-Hadid taken circa 1916

built in several directions. Still, the architectural style in the suburbs was similar to that inside the walls. Buildings had a familiar look and shape and, typically, they featured courtyards surrounded by high walls.

In 2007, there was an effort to reveal part of the western wall of the city, which was covered by a number of illegal structures.

2

Visiting the Citadel

Two days later, before 9:00 AM, Kamal accompanied his son on a visit to the Citadel of Aleppo. They went through modern streets that were laid out decades ago. Along the way, whenever they saw a landmark, Kamal provided a brief explanation—or a longer explanation if he was waiting for a red light to turn green. Tamim received his father's explanations with silence and understanding, though sometimes he would ask for more information about certain landmarks.

Tamim, the old city starts here. These are its boundaries, where the ancient walls once stood. Now, though, the walls and the gates where pedestrians and vehicles entered the old city are gone. On our right, for example, is the location where Bab al-Jinan used to stand, and on the left is where Bab al-Faraj once stood.

Are there any ancient gates still standing? Can we see them?

I will answer your question after I find a spot to park our car. Now, we'll get into this side street. We would probably find a spot there especially this early in the morning. Oh! That's it. We'll park here.

The two got out of the car and walked toward the Grand Mosque. Tamim asked his father to continue with his narration.

Dad, you were going to tell me about the gates that are still standing.

Citadel entrance towers, the larger tower houses the Throne Hall

There are five gates still in existence. Some are in a good condition and we will visit them soon. Look at the end of this street and you can see the Grand Mosque with its beautiful square minaret. Recently, restoration work in the mosque has been completed. We'll also pay it a visit soon.

Dad, what does "restoration" mean?

I will explain it to you later.

They continued walking east. The slope of the Citadel appeared to them at the end of the street. Tamim's father said:

Tamim stared at a part of the Citadel's slope that was visible to him. It was covered with

Description of Aleppo Citadel

The Citadel of Aleppo is located nearly at the center of the old city of Aleppo. It stands on a hill with sloping sides. The Citadel is about 35 meters (115 feet) higher than the surrounding city. It has an oval plan with small and large diameters of about 170×295 meters (560×970 feet). The hill is partly formed of a natural rock. Its upper part, with an altitude of about 15 meters (49 feet), consists of the ruins and remains of successive cultures. Above the hill are walls, about 900 meters (2,950 feet) long. The walls have different projections and recesses in their facades and heights, adding an attractive variety to the Citadel's architectural majesty. The walls also have arrows-slits and defensive towers. There are two advance defense towers in the northern and southern slopes of the Citadel. There is also a moat dug 10 meters (33 feet) deep below the level of the surrounding city. The Citadel is linked to the city by caves and secret passageways.

The Citadel always astounds its visitors when they see it for the first time. It is one of the wonders of Arab defense fortifications. The Citadel is the crown symbol of the city of Aleppo, used as the city's emblem and in the logo of the University of Aleppo. It overlooks the adjacent city from every point and angle of its perimeter walls and watches over a charming background of domes, minarets, monuments, and buildings within the unique urban fabric of the Old City of Aleppo.

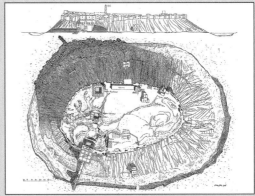

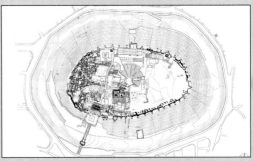

Citadel plans from 1954 (top) and 2005 (above)

City of Aleppo, University of Aleppo, and Baron's Hotel logos

green grass. At the top, some of the Citadel's fortifications and towers could be seen. When they reached the end of the street, they turned left. Now the whole Citadel was in view.

 Oh my God! Is it the Citadel of Aleppo? It's huge! Look at the stone walls! Can we climb up to it?

Five minutes later, they were standing at the curb, at the entrance to this monument.

Tamim, look. Here is the entrance tower. And, where we are standing now, on the street . . . well there is a project to keep cars from driving around the Citadel. This part will be paved with new stone and used only by pedestrians.

Tamim was observing the majestic Citadel as a tangible reality with his little eyes. He was silently staring at its slope, upper walls, and towers at the top. However, more questions were stirring through his young mind.

Tamim observed the majestic Citadel. He was silently staring at its slope, upper walls, and towers at the top. However, more questions were stirring in his young mind.

Tamim and his father started ascending the wide stairway of the Citadel to get to its entrance tower. The father bought two tickets at the gate, and the ticket-office man handed them a brochure and welcomed them. *"Ahlen wasahlen!"* he said. "You are welcome."

Tamim found in the brochure a floor plan of the Citadel and a brief history. They continued walking up the stone entry bridge until they reached the main walls. Tamim turned around to look at the view. Suddenly, he shouted, pointing to a building on the horizon on the right of the stairway below them:

Dad, what is that striped building over there, with a dome on top? It has rows of dark stone and light colored stone. How beautiful it is!

Hammam Yalbugha al-Nasseri viewed from Citadel stairs

His father smiled and repeated the word "striped," then he said:

This is the *Hammam Yalbugha al-Nasseri*, the Yalbugha bath. We'll visit it one day. We might even have a bath in it.

Really, Dad? When will that be?

Soon, God willing.

Tamim turned back to the Citadel, raised his head, and looked at the astounding stone entry. Some of its upper parts were protruding.

Dad, what are those parts projecting out?

First of all, this is the entrance to the Citadel. They call it al-Bashora. Over it, there are two other floors that we will see later. These protruding parts are al-rawashen (or, if you are talking about one of them, the term is "roshan"). They are like windows where guards keep watch on the entrance from the Defense Hall above the Bashora.
Now, Tamim, look at this enormous gate and its iron door, divided into small square cells. Inside each cell, there is something that looks like a horseshoe, with its opening facing downward. This was believed to bring good luck to the inhabitants of the Citadel. This great iron door is part of three identical gates. In fact, it is the second one among them. The first one is the entrance tower we went through on our way in, but you didn't notice it.

Where is the third one then?

You'll see it yourself, so pay attention and be alert.

Tamim's father pointed to the top of the gate and said:

This gate is called "the Serpents' Gate." Look at that relief above it. It features two serpents, each having two dragon heads with pointed ears. The two serpents are carved on each side of the entrance arch, totaling four in number. They are entwined in a pattern that mirrors the arch itself.

Tamim examined the carved design with fascination. The two went through the gate and found themselves in a huge space with a high vaulted ceiling built of stone.

We are now in *al-Bashora*, the Citadel entrance.

The Serpents' Gate to al-Bashora

Interior of al-Bashora

Tamim's father pointed to the top of the gate leading out of *al-Bashora*, deeper into the Citadel. He said to Tamim:

 Look over this next gate. What do you see?

I see a relief image of two lions facing each other.

Yes, indeed. They are also carved on a masonry block. Between them is a lily flower, the emblem of the Ayyubid State.

The Ayyubid State, when did it exist?

It was about 800 years ago, founded by Salah al-Din al-Ayyubi. However, several of the features created by the Ayyubids date back to the king Al-Zaher Ghazi bin Salah al-Din who died in 1216. He was the third son of general Salah al-Din who led the Arab armies against the Crusaders.

Then both of them went through the gate into another space, vaulted and built in the same way as the previous one. On the left side there were narrow slits.

Dad, what are these narrow windows?

Archers stood behind these narrow windows and shot their arrows down onto the assailants below. Notice, Tamim, how this space, like the one before it, abruptly bends, changing its path in a right angle.

Why it is not straight all the way?

This is another defense technique. If an attacker brings a battering ram to attack the iron-clad doors, he will be unable to get a straight run at it because the door is around a corner. This zig zag layout is typical of many other fortresses all over the world.

Kamal and his son walked farther through *al-Bashora*. Kamal went on explaining what they saw, but when he neglected some details, Tamim would hurry to ask him:

Dad, what are those openings up there?

He was pointing to openings high up in *al-Bashora*'s vaulted ceiling. Some were round while others were square. They had interlaced metal bars erected on them like grills and forming little square spaces.

This is also another defense technique.

How so, Dad?

Above *al-Bashora* there is the Great Defense Hall, which we will see on our way out of the Citadel. From this room, defenders could pour hot oil or boiling water to those below who attacked the iron-clad doors. As for those interlaced metal bars, they are for keeping defenders or soldiers from falling down while walking in the darkness in the Defense Hall.

The two kept on walking up the entry passages until they reached a huge gate with two large open shutters. Tamim noticed something and shouted:

Oh, look! Aren't these gate doors the third set of the Citadel gates? Here are the square iron cells on the doors with a horseshoe in each square.

Bravo, Tamim! It is indeed the third gate. Now, have a look, Tamim, at the sides of this masonry opening. These are carved heads of two lions. One is called the

The square iron cells on Citadel gate doors

laughing lion, the other the crying lion. Before you walk farther, look behind you at this high platform, which looks like a grave, all covered up with green cloth.

👦 Yeah Dad, what is this?

👨 This is the shrine of *al-Khidr*, a most venerated saint in the Christian tradition[1].

---

1 The Christians of the Orient believe that he is Mar Gergeos who is called "Saint George" in the West.

People of Aleppo believe that on his travels he passed by the Citadel and gave it a blessing. The care given to his shrine indicates their desire to solicit further blessings and continued protection for the Citadel.

Tamim and his father continued walking to the end of a long corridor with spaces of high platforms on its sides, as if they were masonry benches or *mastabas*. On some of them were heaps of stone and metal balls.

👦 Dad, what are those balls?

👨 They are stone balls, hewed from different types of stone, or metal balls cast from molten metal to form this spherical shape. They are thrown by catapults or mangonels at the enemy. These are the weapons that were used in the past to defend against enemies and assailants. They were even used in attacks against other walled fortresses and cities. We will see more of them later in the Citadel's Weapons Museum.

They proceeded to an open-air yard and continued walking up another long outdoor walkway called the "main road" of the Citadel.

A Brief History of the Citadel

The history of the Citadel is linked to the history of the city of Aleppo. The hill on which the Citadel stands might have been used as a defense site since the establishment of the City thousands of years ago. Some believe the Citadel had been built by Seleucus Nicator (301–281 BC), a Greek king and one of Alexander the Great's military leaders, in the Hellenistic period. Excavations that took place in the Citadel recently, however, have proven that it has a history much older than that. According to the discoveries, it is probably built on a temple from the late Hittite period (the second and first millennium BC).

The first parts of the Citadel's walls might have been built during the Greek or Roman period. Later, the Byzantines restored the fortifications and added a cistern and other items that made the Citadel a strong defense site. It took the surrounding Arab armies months of siege to force the Byzantines inside its walls to surrender.

Successive kings paid attention to building the Citadel and its fortifications, and often made new additions. Some of the most notable:

In 1146, Nur al-Din Zengi erected many buildings in the Citadel, and installed the iron doors on its gates. He made a race course, planted it with grass, and called it "the Green Race Course." He also covered some of its surrounding slopes with stone cladding. Most of the improvements, splendor, and fortifications are due to his work.

When al-Zaher Ghazi, son of Saladin, ruled it in about 1186, he introduced many modifications, additions, fortifications, and improvements. He built a large water cistern as well as grain silos. He demolished the defense tower (al-Bashora) over the slope of the Citadel and rebuilt it with massive stones. He lifted the entrance gate to its current level and built on it two unrivaled towers linked by a bridge that led to the body of the Citadel. He also created five buildings with vaulted

Illustration by British artist Drumond, 1770

ceilings and small arches. He installed iron doors and assigned resting areas for soldiers and statesmen. He also dug a well in the Citadel's depth, known as the Ayyubid Well (or al-Satura), and built in it a water reservoir.

He also built Dar al-Eez, "House of Glory" (the Royal Palace), and around it built houses, rooms, baths, gardens, and places for clerks and soldiers. The Gate of the palace's entrance had a great arch over it, ornamented with muqarnas or multiple nested alcoves.

Some of the buildings in the Citadel were set on fire and some were destroyed when the Tatars seized the citadel in 1259. They destroyed its walls and most of its buildings. They also burned down the two mosques within it. In 1290, the Mamluks restored the Citadel and made it the headquarters of the governor once again, until Tamerlane entered it in 1400 and devastated what had been repaired and restored.

The Mamluk King Al-Ashraf-Khalil bin Qala'un renovated the Citadel in 1291. Then Prince Saif al-Din came to it as Sultan al-Nasser bin Barqook's deputy. He rebuilt what had been destroyed and made additions to it. It was in that period that the Citadel witnessed renovations on a large scale.

The Mamluk Prince Jukum rebuilt the two advance towers (the northern and the southern) in the slope of the Citadel. Sultan Qansuh al-Ghuri (one of the last Mamluk Sultans) renovated them, and it is believed that the entrance of each tower was linked to the Citadel by a secret vaulted passageway.

In 1417 Sultan Mu'ayyed Shaykh roofed the Throne Hall, whose walls had been previously built by Prince Jukum, and restored in the reign of Qaitbay. At the beginning of the 16th century, Qansuh al-Ghuri renovated the walls and replaced the ceiling of the Throne Hall with nine domes. Unfortunately, it was destroyed in the severe earthquake that hit Aleppo in 1822, which harmed the Citadel's walls as well.

During the Ottoman period, the Citadel was used primarily as a barracks for soldiers. When Ibrahim Pasha (son of Mohammad Ali Pasha of Egypt) occupied Aleppo in 1831, he built a barracks in the northern section of the Citadel's crown, known to this day by his name. This is a rectangular building, part of which is used today as the Citadel Museum.

Today, the Citadel is a tourist attraction. Sad to say, a lot of restoration work will be required after the current conflict is over.

Tamim noticed a small group of people right by the beginning of the main road. They had different features and unusual attire. They were gathered around a person who seemed to be their leader, who was talking to them in a language that wasn't Arabic. They were standing in front of a sign-board of the map of the Citadel. Tamim asked:

Dad, who are those people?

They are tourists. You'll see many of them in the Citadel, either in groups or as individuals. The person who is talking to them is the tour guide, explaining to them about the Citadel in their native language. Tourists come from all over the world to know more about the Citadel and the Old City of Aleppo.

The ruins by the main road in the

Dad, this man is their tour guide just like you are my guide, right?

Yes Tamim, but there is a difference between that guide and me. I am your Dad. So you can ask me whatever you want and whenever you want.

The two smiled, and Tamim's father said:

Tamim, come this way.

Then they went under an arched gate to the right of the road and walked through a long passageway with vaulted ceilings until they arrived at a narrow door. They went through it and found themselves in front of a narrow staircase leading down to a huge space. As they reached the bottom, Tamim raised his head up and asked:

Dad, what is this place?

It is called "The Byzantine Hall." Its ceiling is made of sun baked clay bricks. Look, Tamim, isn't this an unusual style of construction in the Citadel! You'll notice that many of the buildings in the Citadel are built with stone. It is true that the enormous pillars supporting this ceiling are made of stone, but look at the roof — it's built in a cross-vault style with clay bricks. This space might have been used as a water cistern. Tamim, come here now and look at this narrow passageway with a staircase leading down.

The two stood looking down at a gloomy space, lit by a faint lamp.

This space underneath is a prison for torture, where the prisoners were left to suffer darkness, starvation, or even death! People of Aleppo call it "the Blood Prison."

They went back out into the light again on the main road of the Citadel, and continued their tour, along paths specified for tourists in the site map given to them at the entry point. The paths wandered here and there. Tamim's father kept explaining, and sometimes answering his son's questions. They reached a high point on the edge of the Citadel's crown near its western walls and stood on a flat surface where another group of tourists was standing. They saw from a short distance the defense towers dotted along the walls encircling the Citadel. Tamim's father said:

Tamim, come and have a look from here.

Observing the Old City from the Citadel walls

This is the City of Aleppo.

Tamim looked in amazement and said:

 Oh my God! It's huge! How beautiful! What are those buildings? How pretty those minarets are! Are those houses occupied?

 Seeing the Old City, and the whole of Aleppo, from this high point is more panoramic and attractive. Now, look there at the arched opening in that building on the side street. It is the entrance to the Medina *souk*, which we will visit later. We'll also pay a visit to some other houses and buildings in Old Aleppo.

Tamim and his father wandered through the ruins of dwellings with remnants of walls and floors. Kamal provided an explanation about the site:

 Tamim, we are here now on the western side of the Citadel. There used to be houses here for some people who were close to the ruler of the Citadel. Most of these buildings were constructed during the Ottoman period, but they were all destroyed. Nothing is left except these ruins of their walls, as you can see.

 Who destroyed them, and how?

 They were destroyed by a devastating earthquake that shook Aleppo in 1822.

They continued their tour, passing through the Great Mosque of the Citadel. When they left the Mosque, they went up a few steps to a vast open area, then turned into a rectangular building on its left. That building was the

The main road going north towards the Citadel's Great Mosque

Citadel Museum, where they saw a model of the Citadel. Tamim said in astonishment:

Is this the Citadel?

Yes, Tamim, it is as if you're observing it from an airplane. It is 200 times smaller than its actual size.

It looks like the aerial view I saw with your papers and photos. But today I see it bigger here, even though I am inside it.

Out of his pocket, his father took something that looked like a pen, a small laser, which sent out a red beam of light wherever he pointed it. He used it to point to Ibrahim Pasha's Barracks on the model, which included the Museum and Visitors Centre.

The father went on pointing at other groups of buildings on the model.

This is the entrance to *al-Satura*; it is the water source for the Citadel. A staircase inside it leads to a freshwater well called the Ayyubid Well. The well is 191 steps down, in a building covered with earth on top, but its lower parts are carved in the rock. The building style of this *Satura* is quite interesting and shows how precise the engineering was 800 years ago. Maybe we'll visit the *Satura* some other time when it's open to the public.

Tamim's father pointed out other places on the model with his red pointer.

This is the Great Mosque, which we just visited. This is the site of the Hittite

What has been taking place in the Citadel of Aleppo and its surrounding area since 2000?

In 2000, the Aga Khan Historic Cities Support Program, in cooperation with the Syrian Directorate General for Antiquities and Museums, initiated qualitative work on the preservation, restoration, and rehabilitation of the Citadel of Aleppo as a tourist site. In 2002 another agreement was signed, between the Historic Cities Support Program and the Directorate of the Old

traffic problems around the Citadel, providing parking facilities, improving façades of nearby buildings, and encouraging tourist-related development in ways that most benefit neighboring areas. Also, they studied the best way to car for the infrastructure of local streets. A related community development program look at economic and social concerns.

City of Aleppo, for preparing a comprehensive urban study for an important vital program—the development of the area surrounding the Citadel of Aleppo ("The Citadel of Aleppo Perimeter Project"), treating it as an integral part of the site of the Citadel itself. Implemented in 2006, the study deals with a number of issues such as

After the completion of these and other restoration efforts, the Citadel became more prominent internationally and drew more tourists. To develop a steady source of income for maintenance and restoration purposes, a number of individuals formed a private, non-governmental organization, "Aleppo Citadel Friends," to promote public collaboration in caring for the Citadel and the surrounding areas, in addition to the efforts carried out by the government.

Some of the ACF's goals are:

Cooperation with the Directorate of Antiquities and Museums and the Directorate of the Old City of Aleppo (in the Aleppo City Council) to improve

Development of viable economic data and cultural assets for the Citadel and its surrounding area, by creating guaranteed investment incomes to cover the costs of projects to protecting and preserving this monument.

Basalt reliefs discovered in the Hittite temple from 1996 to 2006

the Citadel of Aleppo and its surrounding area through a planned and organized work, and to highlight its historical and contemporary stature as a national monument.

Cooperation with the Directorate of Tourism in promoting tourists' awareness of the Citadel and its surrounding area.

أصدقاء قلعة حلب

Aleppo Citadel Friends

The Society of "Aleppo Citadel Friends" was announced in the last quarter of 2006 under the non-profit organization number 2050; its website is: www.aleppocitadelfriends.org

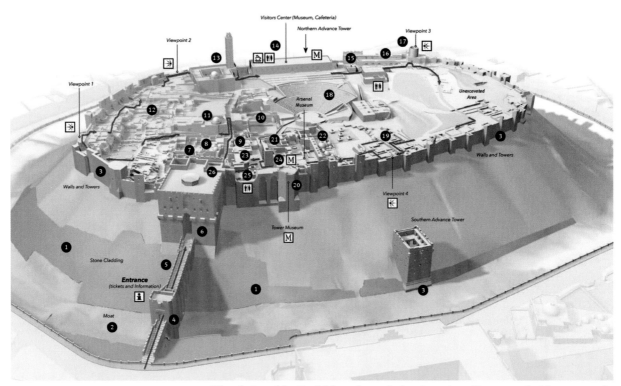

Virtual view of the Citadel from the south showing points of interest and visitors tour paths

temple that was discovered below in the central section of the Citadel. It is turned now into a covered museum to receive tourists. One of the next things on our list, after getting out of here, we'll visit the Ayyubid complex, which includes the Royal Palace and its facilities.

They walked around inside the museum, looking at the display of antique finds that had been unearthed from the Citadel hill.

1. Stone cladding of slopes
2. Moat
3. Walls and towers including advance towers
4. First Entrance tower
5. Bridge
6. Main entrance tower
7. Market
8. Public Bath
9. Byzantine Hall
10. Storm God excavations
11. Lower Mosque
12. Ottoman residential area ruins
13. Great Mosque
14. Ibrahim Pasha barracks
15. Satura (Ayyubid well)
16. Fortifications study excavations
17. Ottoman Windmill
18. Modern amphitheater
19. Ayyubid cistern
20. Mamluk tower/ Tower Museum
21. Ayyubid Palace
22. Mamluk Bath
23. Salty Satura
24. The Arsenal/Museum
25. Al-Tawashi Palace
26. Throne Hall

Hittite basalt relief

Then, they left the museum and walked eastward. Tamim's father pointed to the actual site of the *Satura or well and reservoir*. After that, they continued their way in the same direction and saw a cylinder-shaped building.

Tamim asked:

Dad, what is this building?

It is a windmill. It was built in the Ottoman period and was used for grinding wheat — using wind as a source of power. Its top part crumbled with the passage of time and that cylinder-shaped building is all that is left. It has been restored and rehabilitated, and today it serves as a viewpoint. Let's climb up to it.

They went up through a metal staircase and reached the windmill's terrace first. Then, they continued going up through an internal staircase and reached its peak. Tamim looked around and was delighted to find himself in this spectacular and unique spot, where he could see the city from this high point in the Citadel from an angle different from those he had seen earlier. He could also see the other side of the Citadel's crown. He felt he was the master of the whole scene— the master of all the views around him!

They climbed down, heading south to the Ayyubid complex. Tamim saw a huge outdoor space with a stage area in front of it. He asked his father:

Dad, what is this?

It is an outdoor amphitheater, a recent addition to the Citadel. The Citadel was originally a military establishment, and this theatre was added to host music and theater on summer days! It was constructed in the early 1980s. They should post a notice to inform visitors that it is a modern amphitheater and has no connection with the Citadel or its history.

 What was this area earlier, before the performance space?

 It was used for horse exercise and racing. It was called "The Green Racecourse."

He continued to explain the sites and buildings in the Citadel as they passed by them in the last part of their tour.

 This is the Royal Palace, and that is *al-Tawashi* Palace. (*Al-Tawashi* is the head of the king's servants.) Here is the building of *al-Zardkhana* (the Arsenal), where the weapons and coats of mail used in wars 800 years ago were made. Today, this building is used as a museum for weapons discovered in different places inside the Citadel.

Down the secret stairway

On their way out, Tamim and his father visited the Throne Hall, built in the Mamluk period. Its roof originally had nine domes, but the hall was destroyed in the devastating earthquake that hit the region in 1822. It was re-roofed

Detail of 1770 illustration showing original 9 domes

again in the 1960s in a modern construction technique adopting the flat roof style.

Then they went down to the Great Defense Hall, where they found a secret staircase and followed it down. At the bottom, much to his surprise and delight, Tamim found himself once again in *al-Bashora*, where their visit to the Citadel had started.

They left the Citadel by going down the stairway of the bridge to its entrance tower. Tamim turned back to have a look at the huge tower that contained *al-Bashora*, the Great Defense Hall, and the Throne Hall on top. He said to his father:

Dad, please take a photo of me from here with that amazing tower behind me.

Tamim was not alone in that desire. Many visitors to the Citadel like to take photos in this spot. Tamim told his father that the visit was wonderful, and described the Citadel as great! But there was a mischievous smile on his face when he asked his father:

Dad, did we visit everything in the Citadel on our tour today?

No, Tamim. I promise to bring you back here for another visit, so that you'll understand it better and see other buildings, other angles, and sites. But we didn't have enough time to see all of it today, in one visit.

Dad, time passed by so quickly, didn't it?

School children in front of the Citadel stairs

Courtyard of the Great Mosque, by Wahbi Al-Hariri-Rifai, circa 1990 (above), and interior view (below)

3

Visiting the Medina *Souks*

Tamim's father fulfilled his promise to his son, and decided to take him on another tour to the Old *Souks* (markets), which the natives of Aleppo call the Medina. In the morning, they set out toward the Great Mosque, adjacent to the *Souks*, as the starting point to this tour.

They found a parking spot for their car on a side street, then walked until they reached the entrance of the mosque, which was located on the left side of one of the souks. The wall of the mosque was high and built with old large stones, bearing witness to more than ten centuries of history.

The courtyard of the mosque was expansive. It gave a comfortable feeling of spaciousness, in stark contrast with the crowded areas, crammed buildings, and traffic on the narrow streets they saw outside the mosque.

Tamim's mind wandered, while his small body looked calm. He said to his father:

Who built this mosque, Dad?

The answer to this question isn't just one word or one name. This place you see with all its fine details today is the result of historical accumulations. It reflects the contributions of the different periods Aleppo has gone through since the first stones of this structure were laid. This is the case of most historical buildings, such as the Citadel and other structures, here in Aleppo and elsewhere.

Tamim and his father entered the *Qebliyah*, which is the prayer hall located on the south side of the mosque. They headed toward the *minbar* (a high dais inside the mosque) where *al-Khatib* (the speaker) stands to preach his sermons to the folks who come to pray on Friday's congregational prayer or on the two *Eids* (special religious holidays, one after the fasting month of Ramadan, the other after the end of pilgrimage to Mecca).

Courtyard of the Great Mosque with unique square minaret in background

The Great Mosque

* The Umayyad ruler of Aleppo, Suleiman bin Abdul Malek, gave the order to build the Great Mosque in the eighth century, on land that had been a park and cemetery in the Hellenistic period. Known as the "Agora," it's a plaza where people gathered during celebrations and special occasions.

* The area and shape of the mosque as it stands today has been the result of many successive additions, modifications, and restorations to the original building throughout its history, after having endured repeated arson and vandalism.

* The mosque has a square-shaped minaret, engraved with ornaments and calligraphy. It is of exceptional beauty and harmony among all the minarets throughout the Muslim World, dating back to the Seljuk period in the eleventh century. It is 46 meters high, and its square plan measures nearly 5 meters on each side. One takes a staircase of 174 steps to get to its highest balcony.

* In the first half of the twelfth century, Imad al-Din al-Zangi added the eastern arcade to the mosque and widened the courtyard.

* The mihrab (niche), the minbar, the booth, and other additions were built during the Mamluk period late in the thirteenth century. Many additions and repairs were done during that period.

* In the early sixteenth century, the Ottomans continued work on the Mosque; during this time the courtyard of the mosque was tiled with black and yellow stones, in a uniquely ornamental geometric design.

Painting of the Great Mosque minaret, by artist A. J. Weiss

Tamim, look at this beautiful wooden minbar. Notice the artistic geometric ornaments engraved on it. Notice how it is inlaid with ivory.

What's ivory?

His father pointed with his finger at a white material embedded into the wood pattern. It formed a band that interlaced with the wood to make up the precise geometric patterns. The father said:

Ivory is a hard, pure, and rich whitish material, taken from the tusks of elephants.

Who made this minbar, Dad, and when was it built?

It was made by a carpenter from Aleppo, a master craftsman who built it with fine wood during the reign of the Mamluk king al-Nasser Mohammad, toward the end of the thirteenth century. During its history, Aleppo had many artisans who worked in the various fields of building, cladding, and finishing. There were stonemasons, sculptors, carpenters, and painters. You'll see their fine craftsmanship in many of the public buildings and residential houses in Old Aleppo.

Dad, what's that place over there where people are gathered?

Tamim pointed to a place near the minbar surrounded by a cage-like interlaced grill of yellow metal.

It is the shrine of the Prophet Zachariah (peace be upon him). People often come from different places to ask for blessings and forgiveness. Some are locals from the city of Aleppo, while others come from nearby villages. By the way, in the old days, people of Aleppo used to call this mosque "Zachariah Mosque."

Tamim and his father went through the courtyard again before leaving the mosque. Kamal directed his son's attention to the beautiful square minaret that they had seen earlier from outside the mosque, and to the geometrically ornamented tiles of the courtyard with their black and yellow stones. They left the mosque and visited *al-Halawiya* School. Tamim's father explained to his son the history of the School from its early days until the present. Tamim, as usual, kept asking questions about things his father didn't mention, or just to satisfy his curiosity about certain matters.

Al-Halawiya School

* This site was a temple before it became the Cathedral of Aleppo during the Byzantine period. It was built in the fifth century A.D. but destroyed by the Persian king Kisra Anushirwan in the sixth century.

* In the twelfth century, this site was converted into a mosque, and expanded by Nur al-Din al-Zangi toward the middle of the century. It then became a religious school (madrasa).

* Part of the church is still visible at the western side of the mosque's prayer hall. The school contains a wooden mihrab engraved with unique geometric ornaments. It was renovated during the reign of the last Ayyubid king, Yusuf the Second, in the first half of the thirteenth century.

* In its western side, there are eight columns with Corinthian capitals, dating back to the time of the construction of the cathedral.

* At the top of the school entrance, there is an inscription dating back to the days of Nur al-Din al-Zangi, which commemorates his decree to establish the school of Islamic jurisprudence here.

* Al-Madrasa al-Halawiya was restored several times during the Ottoman period.

Decorated wooden miharb in al-Madrasa al-Halawiya (above right) and interior of prayer hall with Corinthian capitals (right)

Then they went south through one of the *souks* that paralleled the Great Mosque wall.

 Tamim, this was called *Souk al-Hada-deen* — the metal smiths' *souk* or market. In the past, blacksmiths would stand in their shops in front of bellows from which fire flared. They would beat the

Aerial view of the Great Mosque showing the courtyard pavement. The skylight openings of the souk appear to the right

hot iron on the anvils to mold it into various objects and tools, which they sold to those who needed them.

Where are those blacksmiths today, Dad?

I think this profession has shrunk considerably, and is probably going to disappear. There are no more blacksmiths in this souk, and these shops now sell other kinds of products and commodities. Nevertheless, we can still find some blacksmiths near *Bab Antakiya*, which we will visit later, or even at *qabu al-Najjar-eene* (the carpenters' vaulted-way) between *al-Byyadah* quarter, on the perimeter of the citadel, and *Bab al-Hadid*.

They walked through winding streets and crossed several intersections. Tamim marveled at what he was seeing. There was a wonderful mix of people, a meeting place of nationalities and races, and a fair for costumes and clothes of all types. Some people stood in front of shops to place orders. Others were buying spices, herb teas, or other kinds of medicinal herbs and plants. Still others were walking quickly, just passing through the souk to some other destination. Vendors stood in their small shops behind wooden partitions, just a little higher than the floor of the souk. The variety of goods in these shops was amazing. Indeed, some of these souks housed shops that all sold the same kind of merchandise, making them into unified commercial units.

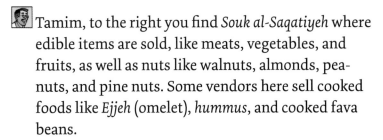 Look Tamim, this is *Souk al-Hibal* (the rope market) and to the right you find *Souk al-Jinfas* (the jute and canvas market).

They passed through a narrow pathway to a long, straight, wide souk — the main core or the central part of the souks.

Tamim, to the right you find *Souk al-Saqatiyeh* where edible items are sold, like meats, vegetables, and fruits, as well as nuts like walnuts, almonds, peanuts, and pine nuts. Some vendors here sell cooked foods like *Ejjeh* (omelet), *hummus*, and cooked fava beans.

Does this souk go much further ahead, Dad?

It goes straight all the way to the Antioch Gate to the west, and to the east it continues till it reaches its end.

What's at the end of this souk, Dad?

I won't tell you now. Let it be a surprise! You'll see for yourself.

During their walk through the souk, Tamim's father asked his son to lift his head up, and said:

Souk al-Hibal (the rope market)

Honey, dates, nuts, and olives in Souk al-Saqatiyeh

Souk Istanbul

At Souk al-Attareen

 Tamim, look at the ceiling of this souk. It is built from a stone vault in the shape of a continuous arch. This was the old way of roofing, if not the oldest way. Back in the old days, it was not possible to cover large spaces with flat and straight roofs.

 Isn't that like the roof of the *Bashora* we saw in the Citadel?

 That's right, Tamim. You'll see it in other places as well.

Moments later, Tamim asked:

 What's that strange smell Dad? It's an amazing fragrance!

 You're right, Tamim. You'll always smell it whenever you visit this souk or pass through it later. You'll be able to tell as soon as you get to it. You're now at *Souk al-Attareen* (the perfumers' market). This aroma is a blend of the fragrances of spices, peppers, perfumes, and medicinal herbs, among other things. Some are local; others are imported. Now look at the people in this souk. Look at the vendors' welcoming faces and the customers who come from all over the world to buy what they believe are unique and rare products that can be found only in this souk. They are proud of their purchases. They feel happy coming to this place to shop. Coming here shows that they have good taste in cooking and are discriminating in what flavors they use in their

Under the skylights of Souk al-Draa (the fabrics market)

Dad, look, aren't those tourists?

Yes, Tamim, you'll find a lot of them here, as individuals or in groups. This man in front of the shop here is probably buying an Aleppian spice mixture or some imported saffron; and this woman, I think, is going to buy a tablecloth with oriental designs. The vendor behind the counter is opening these covers one after another, believing he is helping her make a selection, but he may be confusing her instead with the variety of textiles, designs, and colors. At the end, I think, she's going to buy any of these covers because all of them are beautiful. The one she'll buy will be a beautiful Aleppian souvenir that she'll take back home and treasure.

But how do the vendors communicate with the tourists, what language do they speak with them?

Listen, Tamim, this vendor is speaking English with a tourist, and you'll hear others speaking French. Although their language may not be very good, it is enough for a simple dialogue and for making a sale. The good vendor is the

food. Look at those women over there. They come from the modern parts of Aleppo to buy spices, flavors, and other things. They can be satisfied only with what they buy from this market, *Souk al-Mdeene.*

one who sells the most. He is the one who knows a foreign language to converse with tourists.

Tamim's father went on explaining details about the shops they were passing by.

 This branch here is the old Souk of Istanbul where beautiful textiles for ladies are sold. Women come to this souk to choose fabrics to make dresses for special occasions. The large variety here, the different types of textiles, and the assortment of colors make shopping an enjoyable experience, and reflect the moods and different tastes of the buyers.

Souk Haraj

They walked toward the east and straight through the souk. Every now and then, they would enter a side-branch of the souk.

 This here is *Souk al-Draa*, where tailors sell wool fabrics (also called broadcloth) and tailor it for their customers. That over there is *Souk al-Cotton*, from there to the left *al-Balestan* souk branches off. From this side here, we can enter to *Kayseriet al-Hakakeen*, and this souk is called *Souk al-Dahsheh* (Astonishment Market!).

Wait, Dad, not so fast. I want to know something here. What do they sell at *Souk al-Balestan*? Also, what is *Kayseriet al-Hakakeen*, and what's in it?

Tamim's father grasped his son's hand and took him to *Souk al-Balestan*:

The old Souk Istanbul

At *Souk al-Balestan*, they sell fine handcrafted carpets made from pure wool or silk. They are exquisitely made with wonderful designs and fascinating colors. Some are imported from Persia or *Blad al-Ajam* (the name Aleppians use for old Iran); others come from Central Asia, while some are locally made.

Kamal pointed to a souk intersecting with *Souk al-Balestan*, namely *Souk Haraj*, where they sold the same type of merchandise. Then they headed toward *Kayseriet al-Hakakeen*, going through the Goldsmiths' souk.

This here is an aggregation of small workshops for the goldsmiths and jewelers who make creative designs of gold, and sometimes silver, jewelry. The word *'al-Hakakeen'* means those who rub things; it refers to goldsmiths, who rub the metal to see if it's gold, silver, or something else. They melt gold and cast it into beautiful designs. The Goldsmith souk expanded and branched off into shops that sell gold jewelry in adjacent souks.

They returned to the main core of the souk, and Tamim went on with his questions, always curious to learn more.

But, Dad, you haven't told me, what do they sell at *Souk al-Dahsheh*?

Back in the old days, the *Souk al-Dahsheh* was full of exotic goods from far away: eastern goods that merchants brought from abroad in caravans on the Silk Road coming from the east, where Aleppo was an important stop, and western goods imported on ships coming from Europe. Over time, this souk lost its importance, and the merchandise that used to be sold here changed. However, it kept its old name, *Souk al-Dahsheh*.

Well, Dad, I think all the old souks we've been to are astonishing. Aren't they? All of them should be called souks *al-Dahsheh*.

Good observation, Tamim! They are astonishing indeed even to those who come here often.

After a few steps he said:

We are now at *Souk al-Zarb. Al-Zarb* is a barrier made of straight reed sticks with black goatskin twines tying the sticks together. Bedouins who came from *al-Badiya* (the Syrian Desert) often bought these barriers here to use as screens for their tents.

Souk al-Hakakeen (the goldsmith's market)

Where are the shops that sell those Zarb barriers?

Well, Tamim, over time, this craft became extinct too. The Bedouins started to make screens for their tents out of straw or plastic mats. Nevertheless, the souk still retains the name *al-Zarb*. Mind you, some shops still sell tent equipment for the Bedouins' needs.

At the end of *Souk al-Zarb*, daylight shone through an arched opening leading to the outside space. They went out through it, and passed to the light. Tamim shouted in amazement:

Oh, God! This is the Citadel we see here, Dad, isn't it? This is the surprise you told me about when we were inside the Souk. We've reached its end now.

*   *   *

What do you say about going back now, Tamim?

Has our visit finished today?

I meant, let's return toward the car now, and on our way, we will see other things, which will be part of our tour today.

Imagined painting in front of Khairbek Khan, by A. J. Weiss

Souk al-Attareen

Decorative masonry work of Khan al-Saboun elevation

They turned left two times, and walked on, leaving the citadel behind them. They descended a long inclined street, from which cars came up toward the citadel. The street had modern buildings with many stories on both sides. Tamim asked:

Are we still here in Old Aleppo, Dad?

We are at the oldest places in Old Aleppo, especially because we are near the Citadel. But a few decades ago, the government decided to open this street, and they made a cut through the traditional fabric of the Old City which devastated many houses and removed public buildings, alleys, and lanes.

When did that happen, Dad?

A little more than half a century ago, when the people of Aleppo were not thinking about protecting their Old City yet or even about preserving their heritage. Instead, their aim at that time was to follow modernity and to renew the whole City of Aleppo, including its oldest areas.

They passed near a high wall on the left side of the street. Kamal said:

Tamim, look at this high wall. It is a new, but built according to the old way of construction, to cover the bits of *Khan al-Wazir* that became exposed when they cut this street through here.

Where is *Khan al-Wazir* now?

We thank God that **cutting the street** sliced only a small part of the *Khan*'s side that parallels the street. We are close and will visit it now.

Tamim observed the beautiful facade of *Khan al-Wazir* and its entrance; the masonry ornaments and the method of building fascinated him.

What a beautiful facade! I think I've seen something similar to it someplace else. This isn't the first time I see a striped facade in two colors of stone.

Try to remember what we saw on our previous visit. This facade with bands, or "stripes" as you called it, is

Interior courtyard of Khan al-Wazir depicted on an old postcard

characterized by alternating black and yellow courses of stone, known as *Ablaq*. It is an old style of building regal facades, and was popular during the Mamluk and Ottoman periods. There are some facades of buildings built with *Ablaq* style preserved here in Aleppo, and it was used at the same periods in Damascus, Cairo, and other cities in the Middle East.

Yes, Dad: I remember where I saw a facade like this one. Didn't the entrance of the Royal Palace in the Citadel have a striped facade like this? I also saw one like this at the perimeter of the Citadel.

Bravo, Tamim! Yes, indeed. It was the front facade of the

The Old Souks of Aleppo (Al-Medina)

* Building of the Souks started out near the plaza (Agora) where the Great Mosque is now located. Merchants and people gathered there, exchanging goods and dealing with social and economic concerns important to them. To the south of that location, a straight 750-meter-long road was set up going east–west between the western slope of the Citadel and Bab Antakya. It later became the main core of the souk in the city.

* Many other souks branched off from this straight road (the main core), and other souks ran parallel to it in the vicinity of the Great Mosque.

* The Byzantines destroyed and burned Aleppo and its souks in the tenth century, but they were restored, expanded, and roofed with wood during the Zangid and Ayyubid periods. Hulagu destroyed them again in 1260.

* Residential quarters were established around the main road dating back to the third century BC.

* The souks flourished again at the onset of the Mamluk period, until Tamerlane devastated them in 1400. They were restored and flourished once again. A number of Khans (caravanserais) were set up as accommodations for goods-laden caravans, and to facilitate commercial exchange with traveling merchants. The souks at those times were centers of "wholesale" trade.

* With the beginning of the Ottoman period in the sixteenth century, other Khans were established near the souks, totaling 68 Khans in the eighteenth century (according to Russell*), in addition to a number of public buildings such as mosques, religious schools, and public Hammams (baths). It was during this time that the souks were re-roofed with masonry vaults[†].

* The total length of the old Souks of Aleppo, the main core and its branches, is about 12 kilometers (7.5 miles). They are considered the world's longest covered souks.

* Each souk in the Medina was a specialty market in the sense that it sold a certain kind of merchandise (some still do so even now). For example, this is Souk al-Hibal (ropes) and that is Souk al-Attareen (perfumes and medicinal herbs), and over there is Souk al-Zarb (tent equipment), and that is the Fabric souk, and so on. The number of souks amounts to 37 in total.

V.D. 35   ALEP - Souk des Cordes.

Old photography of Souk al-Hibal (the ropes market)

* *The Medina souks are a huge warehouse for goods and merchandise rarely found elsewhere in the world. The souks are known for their value and variety[††], and distinguished by their age and authenticity. The souks of the Medina are considered an attraction for the local people, residents of Aleppo and others, and for those coming from the suburbs and the countryside, in addition to the tourists who come there at all seasons. They find these souks full of life and activity, and enjoy the variety of goods, the reasonable prices, and pleasant service, all of which add up to a gratifying shopping and touring experience.*

[†] *The Brothers Russell (Alexander and Patrick) were the British community's physicians in Aleppo at the middle of the eighteenth century; they wrote a book titled* The Natural History of Aleppo. *This book is an important reference about the period when they were living in Aleppo; the book was translated into Arabic in the 1990s.*

[††] *The French traveler Chevalier (from the 17th century) mentioned: "you'll find in Aleppo's souks everything, from the straw mat to the pearls."*

In the interior courtyard of Khan al-Wazir

Yalbugha al-Nasseri public hammam, which we saw when we were going up the entrance stairway of the Citadel. Don't forget that we also saw a similar one at the entrance of the Throne Hall in the Citadel. Maybe we'll see others like it elsewhere in old Aleppo.

Tamim and his father then entered the khan through its huge gate. Tamim asked:

What was this place used for, Dad?

Well, Tamim, the *khan*, or caravansary, is a place used primarily for commercial purposes. Its vast courtyard in the center was used for the reception of the trading caravans that came from different countries, when camels and mules were used for carrying imported goods to Aleppo, as they were the only means of transport used at that time. Cars and trucks weren't available yet. Those caravans would unload their cargo here in this courtyard. The merchants who brought the caravans would rent some of the khan's rooms at its ground floor as offices. Here, they carried out their deals and transactions, received customers, and did their accounts, as well as other activities.

Then, pointing with his hand, he said:

Look, Tamim, those are the rooms that surround the khan's courtyard. In addition, the rooms on the first floor, connected by a higher arcade, provided accommodations for the traveling merchants where they could enjoy some quiet and privacy, just like rooms in hotels nowadays. Some would stay in them for months while selling their merchandise and buying other goods from Aleppo to take with them upon returning to their homelands.

Tamim and his father wandered together in the khan's courtyard and saw how the rooms of the commercial exchange and accommodations on the two floors of the khan had been transformed into shops, offices, and workshops.

Some of these rooms, Tamim, are even being used today as offices for doing business deals over the telephone. Recently, the consulate of a European country located its offices on the west side of the khan. And notice how the khan's courtyard has been turned into a parking space for the cars of the khan's merchants, instead of the caravan animals that were used in the past! Tamim, change is an essential part of life. In some cases, matters just impose themselves upon us, and all we can do is adapt to change and accept the power of reality.

As they were heading toward the interior of the khan's facade, Tamim raised his head and said:

Dad, look how beautiful this facade is! Those decorations around the windows are so detailed and delicate.

Tamim, the Aleppian stonemason is an artist by instinct, a sculptor who knows how to deal with stone and how to make it into beautiful things. You'll see in our future visits much of the beauty of stone carving in houses and public buildings in Old Aleppo.

They walked back into the new street heading towards the Great Mosque.

Look, Tamim, this left turn is a side entrance to the Medina souks. We can get through it to the main core of the souks again. To the right here is a different kind of souk, an extension of the Medina souks. People of Aleppo call it "*Al-Sweiqah*" (a diminutive for souk).
Look, here to the left again, this is another side entrance to the Medina souks. It's called "The New Souk of Istanbul." In the past, it housed merchandise imported from Istanbul, but today most of the goods sold here are locally made.
At the Medina souks, you find a large variety of different goods and merchandise. People of Aleppo say: "It has it all, from the needle and pin to the bride's trousseau." Imagine, Tamim, what the Medina souks contain! They are a place where the city's economy is most clearly evident; they are where locally made as well as imported goods and merchandise are sold, a truly unique commercial center, indeed!

Before they left the location, the father said to his son:

Tamim, look to your left here… this is the courtyard of the Great Mosque again, and this is its northern exterior facade, which wasn't there originally. It became necessary to create it, after this street had been opened here. Its architectural elements are derived from the details of the Great Mosque's minaret itself. It was a successful solution by a contemporary Aleppian architect. Tamim, let's head back to the car now. Our tour is over for today, and I think you're tired of walking.

Mamluk emblem (rank) carved on the walls of the courtyard of Khairbek Khan. These emblems, found in may public buildings in Aleppo, represent an official at the court by symbols indicating his governmental work or duty

—◇ (4) ◇—
Visiting *Bab Qinnisreen* (*Qinnisreen* Gate)

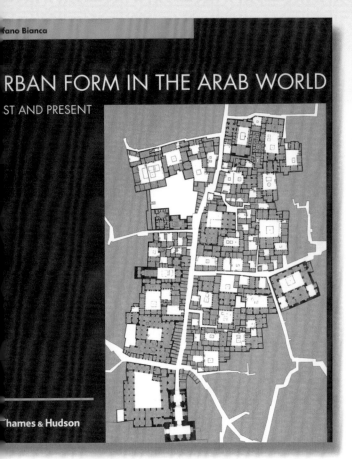

Urban map of Bab Qinnisreen neighborhood appears on the cover of the book "Urban Form in the Arab World"

On another day, Tamim's father took his son by car toward *Bab Qinnisreen*. Along the way, he pointed to his right and said:

Tamim, we'll turn right over here and drive along the Old City limits where the walls and gates once stood. In this place there was a gate called *Bab al-Jinan*, which crumbled and disappeared. These buildings and shops over here were built on top of the walls, covering them up. There is a project to demolish them and unveil the City walls. To our left, you'll see *Bab Antakiya* (Antioch Gate), which is still standing. There are two towers, one on each side. We'll see the gate and the area behind it on another visit, but now we will head to *Bab Qinnisreen*.

He took a left turn and said:

The City wall once wound up eastward around this part of the city.

Then he slowed the car down and said:

Tamim, look at this brown sign on our left. Can you read it?

Yes, Dad, "The Old City of Aleppo. A World Heritage Site."

Right, Tamim. Old Aleppo is now listed by UNESCO as a world heritage site. This means that the whole world has an interest in preserving it. There are plenty of similar brown signs distributed in and around the Old City. Look to your left, to these two defense towers along the walls. They are in bad condition and need care and restoration.

When they reached the end of the road and got out of the car, Tamim said:

Isn't this gate *Bab Qinnisreen*?

Yes, it is. Through this gate, people in the past would get in and out of the city. Like any other gate, it was closed at night and opened during the daytime, but at times of war, it was always closed to protect the city. Ah, Tamim, before I forget, look to your right towards the south. What do you see?

I see nothing... I mean no building, just raised ground.

Yes, it is an empty land called *"Tallet as-Sawda"* (The Black Hill)[1], with caves underneath. A project is currently underway to set up a beautiful park for entertainment for the inhabitants of adjacent neighborhoods and more. It will surely enhance the value of property and improve the urban environment in its surrounding area.

They walked slowly and went into the gate. Tamim raised his head and said:

---

1 The definition of *Tallet as-Sawda* will come on p. 62.

General view of Bab Qinnisreen neighborhood with Citadel in background

Look at the roof, Dad! Doesn't it look like the roof of the *Bashura* in the Citadel?

Bravo, Tamim! This site here is quiet like the Citadel. Its function is to defend the city. Besides, the vault was the only way of roofing known at that time for such large buildings. Then look here and over there. This place has four gates, each of which used to have two shutters that were closed at night and opened in the daytime.

As if recalling information from a previous visit, Tamim said:

Dad, do you see how this place was also built at a right angle? It's quiet like the *Bashura* of the Citadel of Aleppo. Aren't these arrow-slits as well?

Right, Tamim. Didn't I tell you that you always find this type of plan in defensive sites? This place is just like the Citadel. The soldiers at *Bab Qinnisreen* would defend the city against attackers from here,

Tallet as-Sawda
(The Black Hill) and the Origin of the City

Tallet as-Sawda lies to the west of Qal'et Ashareef quarter and to the south of Bab Qinnisreen. It is relatively higher than the area surrounding it. A number of pottery fragments and dolls were unearthed from this site. Furthermore, some archaeological digs reveal that it is an artificial hill, like any other ancient hill in which layers of different successive civilizations have been found. It is considered one of the earliest centers of settlement in Aleppo, from which construction extended westward.

Tallet as-Sawda contains, deep in its layers, some of Aleppo's caves, which form an extension to the great caves located to its southwest (Al-Maghaier Quarter). These caves were undoubtedly inhabited, evidence of which is the existence of carved rooms, stone benches for sitting, and holes at the top for ventilation (skylights)[†]. Perhaps ancestors of the Aleppians lived in those caves but later abandoned them due to the growth of population and the evolution of construction techniques. They built their dwellings over the hill considered by many researchers as the best location for the beginning of urbanization. Due to a variety of advantages, the earliest cells and quarters of the City started here. Over time, these cells expanded and the construction extended westward and northward toward the river. These cells later acquired an urban form.

The City expanded rapidly, and so did its activities, at a time when the Citadel hill was the sacred religious center of City. This expansion took two directions: westward toward the main water resource, the river, and eastward toward the main worship center, the Citadel hill.

Studies also prove that although the City expanded, it maintained its earliest quarters while new neighborhoods emerged in the north, west, and south, adhering to the strict Hellenistic style in planning. This was evident in the straight and perpendicular roads going in the four cardinal directions. New energies flowed into the City. The fortified citadel hill became the acropolis overlooking the City. Souks emerged and led up to a public square, the 'Agora.' Water was supplied to the City from another source in the east through a canal called the 'Helan canal' dug underground in the rock.

Walls were built around the city for defensive needs, but over the years they either eroded on their own or were often demolished, restored, and extended, until the beginning of the Ottoman period.

Much plunder and destruction took place every time the City was conquered, but it often recuperated and witnessed construction and prosperity afterwards. Aleppo became a great intellectual and religious center over the years. The City expanded and construction extended to other areas. Aleppo became a great city teeming with life, and continues to grow to this day. Unlike other cities, it did not die despite all catastrophes, disasters, and turbulence of time.

† *Khair al-Din al-Asadi described "Al Maghaier" as a carved town in the stone. He was one of the few adventurers who visited it and wrote about it.*

Opening of a cave carved in the rock at Tallet as-Sawda

Aleppo Citadel as it appears from Tallet as-Sawda

and prevent them from entering the city.

They went through the last gate out to daylight and found themselves in front of a long and straight road.

 Tamim, notice how behind each gate in the Old City, you'll find a straight road. It is often a commercial axis with shops and stores on both sides. These usually branch off into alleyways and *zuqaq* leading to residential quarters in the area. We are here in this commercial axis, and in front of us is an example of what we always find after each gate in the Old City. Sometimes you find public buildings such as mosques, schools, and public baths that provide services to people living in the area.

As they walked at a slow pace, Tamim's father greeted shopkeepers and went on with his explanation to his son at every turn or in front of every public building along the axis called "Bab Qinnisreen Street."

This turn leads to a dead end, meaning that there is a house at its end. This is the arched entrance of the alley. The street or alley behind it is called a 'gate.'

Tamim and his father standing in the gate of Bab Qinnisreen

Are we going through this gate today?

We'll put that off for now, since there are a number of houses worth a special visit here. Look to the left. This is another, smaller gate, at the end of which there is a house too. Its owners, along with many others in the Old City, abandoned it a long time ago.

An alleyway in Bab Qinnisreen neighborhood

Why were these houses abandoned, Dad?

Most of the deserted houses were the large houses in the area. That could have been because of changes in the family's order. The extended family is no longer present in one house, as it was in the past when two or three generations lived in the same house. People wanted change. Apartments in the tall buildings that spread around the city became more appealing because of the independence they offered. Anyway, we'll delay talking further about this to some other time. We'll see similar examples when we make other visits. By the way, in the house at the end of this alley, a construction crew is working to convert it into a hotel!

Tamim raised his eyebrows and repeated his father's word in astonishment: 'A hotel!'

The two continued walking, and Tamim's father resumed talking about the buildings and places they saw along the way.

To the right, this *zuqaq* (alleyway) leads to other alleys and quarters. About a hundred meters from here is the *al-Rumi* mosque with its beautiful cylindrical minaret. We will visit it at some other time.

They kept walking in the main axis. Then Tamim's father said:

On the left is the *al-Jawhari* public bath. Now it is deserted too. Its owner uses it as a warehouse or storage place. On the right is the *al-Karimiya* mosque.

Tamim then interrupted his father:

Why was this public bath abandoned, Dad?

Also because of changes in lifestyle. The city expanded, and each apartment in the modern buildings has its own bath. Public baths were no longer economically rewarding, so the owner of this one closed it down.

What do the people of this neighborhood do when they want to have a bath then?

They manage to do so by creating a small bath in a space at their houses or...

The father didn't complete his sentence and pointed to the right.

Tamim look here. We now arrive at the *Bimaristan al-Arghoni*.

What? What do you mean by *Bimaristan*, Dad?

Interior courtyard of a house in Bab Qinnisreen neighborhood now used as

Bimaristan is a hospital. The word is from a Persian origin. *Bimar* means 'patient' and the whole word means 'patients' place' or 'place of health.'

Are we getting in?

Of course. Come with me and look at the Arabic calligraphy inscribed on the stone sign above the entrance gate and the *muqarnas* ornaments above it.

Old photograph of north iwan in the courtyard of Bimaristan al-Arghoni

Bimaristan al-Arghoni courtyard south facade

Tamim raised his gaze, marveling at the beauty of the entrance and the *muqarnas* semi-dome above it.

What does *muqarnas* mean when you described the ornaments above the entrance?

Muqarnas ornament is one of the distinctive features of Islamic architecture. Each single cell of *muqarnas* is like a small niche, usually used in groups and forming rows that are well organized in distribution and structure, next to and over each other. Every group of *muqarnasat* (the plural of *muqarnas*) resembles beautiful beehives, as you see them here. In addition to their aesthetic and ornamental function, they have a specific architectural and constructional function.

We saw these *muqarnasat* in the Citadel,

Tamim rests at the Bimaristan's iwan

Tamim's father started reading what was written on the stone sign. Then they entered, passing two vaulted spaces. They moved to a grand open courtyard in the middle of which was a large rectangular pool. The water was flowing from a fountain in the center and filling the pool. Next to the pool were two wells: at the top of each was a treated flat iron bow with a pulley and rob. The bucket went down to the bottom of the well to bring clean water to the top.

Where does clean water come from, Dad?

It rises from groundwater, which is more than ten meters in depth.

Tamim listened to his father's explanation about the building, the two spaces on its sides with arches at their facades, and other structures around the courtyard. Then he asked his father:

When was this hospital built?

The sign we read over its entrance states that it was built in 755 AH (1354 AD). In other words in the fourteenth century, during the Mamluk period.

You always talk about periods Aleppo went through in history, such as Mamluk,

didn't we Dad? Do you remember?

Yes, Tamim. One was over the royal palace entrance in the citadel and the other was over the Throne Hall entrance there. Excellent, Tamim. Your observation is sharp. You can also find *muqarnasat* on many buildings in Old Aleppo.

Illustration of Old City taken from west of Citadel

Ayyubid, and others. When were those periods, Dad?

Tamim, remind me tomorrow and I'll explain to you a chronological time-line of the periods for Syria in general and Aleppo in particular. Only then will you understand the history of the city, the periods it went through and when those periods were. Let's now get through here.

They entered a narrow passageway and turned left, to find themselves in a small open courtyard. Overlooking the courtyard were windows with interlaced metal grills.

Where are we, Dad?

We are in one of the hospital wards. By the way, I forget to tell you that this hospital was dedicated for patients with mental illnesses.

What are mental illnesses?

Well, my son, the human being is made up of body and soul, or let's just say, body and mind. Just like the human body that becomes ill, so does the mind. In the past our ancestors realized that, so they established a hospital for mental patients where they could be isolated and could receive care and therapy by doctors. The patients' wards were divided into three sections according to their conditions. This ward here was for patients with severe conditions.

Do you mean that they were insane, Dad?

Yes, the patients in this ward were the most dangerous. Therefore, their isolation was stricter.

They went back through the same passage and entered two other wards: one for patients with medium conditions and the other for those with milder cases.

Kamal continued his conversation with Tamim, who was trying to make sense out of all this information.

Bab Qinnisreen
(Qinnisreen Gate) and Adjacent Areas

Bab Qinnisreen is considered one of the most important gates of Old Aleppo, located on its historical wall. Today it is one of the most complete gates of an Islamic Middle Eastern city. It is also where part of the wall going east–west terminates.

Bab Qinnisreen was built during the reign of Saif al-Dawla al-Hamadani (944–975). It was renovated by the king Al-Nasser Mohammad, grandson of Salah al-Din al-Ayyubi (Saladin) in 1256.

In olden times, the gate led to a town called Qinnisreen, southwest of Aleppo. The town no longer exists.

To the south of the gate, facing the city wall, are the "al-Maghaier" and "Tallet as-Sawda" areas with their subterranean natural caves. It is believed that some of these caves stretch beneath Bab Qinnisreen inside the walls area.

An irrigation network was built in the area during the Roman period; it branched off as a tributary from the Helan canal, which supplied Aleppo with water. Aside from that, the inhabitants also depended on building reservoirs (cisterns) to collect rainwater. In addition to that, wells were dug to supply houses with groundwater.

The most important historical buildings within Bab Qinnisreen are:

Early morning view of the road leading to Bab Qinnisreen

Monkli Bugha (Al-Rumi) Mosque was constructed during the Mamluk period in 1366 AD and was renovated and restored over successive periods.

Al-Assadiyya School was established during the Zangid period in 1128 and rebuilt in 1544. It is currently used as a health center for the inhabitants of Bab Qinnisreen and Al-Jallum in Old Aleppo.

Al-Kareemieh Mosque was constructed in the seventh century and renovated in 1256 and then in 1451.

There is still one soap factory left in the area. It produces laurel soap, for which Aleppo is famous.

Al-Arghoni al-Kameli Bimaristan[†] is one of the most important Bimaristans in the Orient. It was built by Aleppo governor Arghon al-Kameli at the command of the Mamluk Sultan al-Nasser

Kalawun in 1354. It was a mental hospital.

Al-Jawhari public bath (Hammam) was established by Akk Bugha al-Jawhari in 1397. It was supplied with water through the Helan canal. It is deserted now.

Khan (caravansary) al-Qadi was established by Aleppo judge Kamal addin al-Maari (known as Ibn Ashehna) in 1450 as a school. It was later converted into a commercial khan.

Al-Shaibani School is located near the end of Bab Qinnisreen's axis, facing north. The use of this building changed several times. One such use was Al-Zajjajia school, up until the Franciscan mission bought it from the al-Shaibani family in the middle of the nineteenth century. They established a vast building that included a monastery, a chapel, and a school annex. The construction started in 1853, and the chapel and the school were put to use in 1879. Then the site was abandoned in 1937 when the chapel and school were moved to another site in the west of modern Aleppo. The state then owned the site and used some of its spaces as a warehouse. Since that time the building has not been maintained. In 2001 restoration and rehabilitation work on the building was started and some of its spaces were used for cultural activities, such as "the permanent exhibition of the rehabilitation processes in the Old City" and

Al-Shaibani marked in red on the map of the Old City

occasional exhibitions of primary school students' paintings from Aleppo (old and modern) in which they express their impressions of what they see in the Old City. Musical concerts, both oriental and classical, are performed in the courtyard when the weather is good.

The area also includes a number of important, spacious, and luxurious houses, considered some of the oldest and most distinguished in the Old City.

The area of Bab Qinnisreen quarter was chosen as the first selection from a group of Old Aleppo quarters to be the pilot project in the rehabilitation of the Old City of Aleppo.

In late 2004, Arab Cities Organization awarded the Architectural Heritage Prize to the Bab Qinnisreen quarter rehabilitation project.

---

† Bimaristan: the ancient name for Hospital. It is of Persian origin.

Do you notice the differences in the architectural design of each ward?

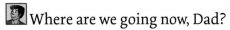Yes, I do.

This ward has the largest courtyard, and the surrounding rooms have their doors open to it. Patients here were allowed to meet and communicate with each other and could meet with visitors. You should know, Tamim, that during the time this hospital was built, the West was in a state of intellectual backwardness, darkness, and ignorance. The mental patients in the West at that time were killed because they were thought to be possessed by the devil and had to be disposed of.

They completed their tour in the *Bimaristan*. Then they went out of its gate and found themselves in the same busy commercial axis they came from.

Where are we going now, Dad?

Tamim, look at this space in front of the *Bimaristan* entrance.

Tamim saw a sign on the opposite wall and read it

It's *Masbane*. What does that mean?

Laurel soap blocks set in rows in the drying hall

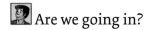It is a soap factory. In this quarter there were three soap factories, but today there is just one.

Are we going in?

It is closed at this time of the year. Soap "cooking" is seasonal. It starts in late fall and early winter. We'll pay a visit around that time, because its production process is worth seeing.

What kind of soap does it produce?

The traditional soap Aleppo is famed for, particularly laurel soap, a specialty of Aleppo.

We do have laurel soap at our home, Dad.

Yes, Tamim. Your mother and I don't use any other soap. It is a natural organic product in which olive oil is used and laurel oil is added to it to give it this gentle appealing scent.

Should I remind you next fall to come here in order to visit the soap factory?

Don't forget to do so, Tamim.

* * *

Bimaristan al-Arghoni with Qayem al-Qanayeh on left side wall

The two continued walking north, passing

by some sites and buildings. Kamal, as usual, was explaining to his son about this small khan (caravansary) and that mosque. Then he drew his son's attention to a small high opening located on the sidewall of the *Bimaristan*. A similar opening was also located on another wall in the busy axis in which they were walking.

Tamim, look at this opening and that one over there.

Tamim raised his small head and asked:

What are these openings and why are they blocked inside? They don't seem to lead to the inside of the building.

They open towards the bottom deep inside the opening where you can see the pottery vertical pipes on the wall. They are connected with an ancient underground aqueduct believed to be from Roman times. These openings you see here and there located at the intersections of alleys and lanes in the Old City are called *Qayem*

Qayem al-Qanayeh with step recesses leading up to opening

al-Qanayeh (the vertical water pipe of the canal).

What is the function of the vertical water pipe? Is it still in operation?

No, Tamim. The aqueduct went out of use decades ago, after completion of projects to supply the old and modern city through metal and concrete pipes bringing water from purification plants and distributing it to houses, where it comes out of taps. Look at these small square gaps arranged side by side leading up to the opening itself.

I was about to ask you about them!

They serve as steps that *al-Qanawati* (the canal custodian) would climb to the top of the opening. The canal custodian is a person responsible for distributing water to houses and dwellings. He reaches to the top of the opening, and opens and closes the pipes according to the amount of water allocated for each house.

"Canal custodian" then is the name of the person who works in the canal. In fact, one of my friends at school has *al-Qanawati* as his family name.

That's right, son. This profession is now extinct, just like many other old professions in Aleppo. All that is left of them is the family names.

*   *   *

They walked along the same busy axis, turning to the right and then to the left, finally reaching a four-way intersection.

Where are we now, Dad?

We're at the end of *Bab Qinnisreen* Street. If we continue walking northward in the same direction, we'll reach the Medina souks.

And from there we'll get to the Citadel, is that right, Dad?

Bravo, Tamim! But let's have a look at this small khan now.

What's the name of this khan, Dad? It is smaller than *Khan al-Wazir*, which we saw on our previous visit.

Some khans are large, while others are small. What prompted me to ask you to take a look at this khan from the inside is not just to know about small khans, as you did about big ones, but to let you know that this khan was built by my great-grandfather, and it is known around here in this area by our family name.

They entered inside the khan and took a general look. Tamim asked.

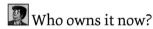 Who owns it now?

Our family is no longer the sole proprietor, as there are other owners now. My brothers and I got some shares of it through inheritance. Come this way, let's turn left. I'll show you a unique place in the Old City.

They walked westward until they reached a wall in the end of the road, which changed the direction of the road to the right, but to the left it led to a huge gate. On the front of that wall a statement read *"Old Aleppo: Continuing Development," The Permanent Exhibition.*

Tamim, come this way. Let's visit this place.

They found themselves in an unusual site. A large and lofty entrance space led to a high corridor supported by cylindrical columns.

Exhibition hall in al-Shaibani School used for temporary exhibits

To the right, it opened onto a vast courtyard or garden. It was full of high trees and surrounded by two-story buildings with windows looking onto the courtyard.

What's this building, Dad? What's this place?

It is a school established by a Franciscan mission. A chapel and monastery were annexed to it. It is known as *al-Shaibani* School or Church.

When was this school built?

Documents say that it was built in the middle of the nineteenth century. Some say it is older than that.

Is the school still here?

No, it was moved elsewhere in the modern part of the city in the first half of the

An old lithograph of the City from Bab Qinnisreen direction

twentieth century. The site was abandoned for a while, and then part of it was used as a warehouse for a governmental institution. Due to its importance and its location and building inside the Old City, a plan was set up to restore it and rehabilitate it to be used for worthwhile and suitable activities. **Restoration work here is almost finished.**

What will the building be used for?

It has been recently selected as a center for cultural activities inside the Old City, serving the inhabitants and attracting people from other areas. The most im-portant function of this place is its role as the permanent exhibition of the rehabilitation project at the Old City of Aleppo. I've recently been informed that a center for rehabilitating and training the inhabitants of the Old City is going to occupy part of the building.

Training for what, Dad?

Young men and women will be given training on some professions. They'll get a chance to learn foreign languages and how to use computers. Anyway, this is a multi-purpose developmental project, with various activities. I'll tell you more about it some other time. Come here this way, Tamim.

They were in a wide corridor with cylindrical columns that opened up to the courtyard in front of them. They turned back and entered a big rectangular hall, in which there were items on display that had been meticulously arranged. Visitors to this exhibition would follow a well-planned route to see everything in the exhibition: wall pictures narrating the story of Old Aleppo and describing its rehabilitation project, models built of old stones taken from a wall of a house in the Old City, an old pool in the middle of the space,

a built model of an *iwan* in an Aleppian
house, and a small model of a distinguished
Aleppian house in the middle of one of the
exhibition sections. On the walls, there were
historical pictures of the site and the school
building in which this permanent exhibition
was housed. A treated hard gypsum model
of the Old City within the walls, at a scale
of 1:500, was displayed in the middle of the
last section of the exhibition. Tamim was
amazed to see Old Aleppo in all its details:
its Citadel was in the middle, surrounded by
the City with its houses, alleys, lanes, quarters, public buildings, and so on.

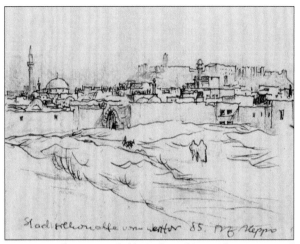

Illustration of Old City by architect Helmut Trauzettel

The whole tour in the exhibition was astonishing to Tamim. It summed up a lot of things
and gave answers to a lot of questions that
were on his mind about Old Aleppo. The iris-
es of his eyes widened when he watched the
model of the Old City in front of him. Then he
asked his father:

*Aleppo Old City model exhibited at Aleppo Museum and at the
Old City permanent exhibition at al-Shaibani School*

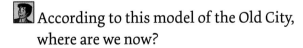 According to this model of the Old City,
where are we now?

Tamim's father took a laser pointer out of
his pocket, pressed on its side, and directed
the laser beam towards a small flag planted
somewhere in the model.

We are here, at this small flag. This is the
street we walked through and then took
a left turn.

Tamim's father pointed the light, tracing the
axial way from *Bab Qinnisreen*; Tamim started talking about some of the details with his

father.

The Citadel isn't far from here, as I can see!

It's a five-minute walk from here, or it may take more if you go through the City souks and walk slowly to enjoy what you see.

Did you say that this is a model of the Old City within the walls?

An alleyway in the Old City

Yes, Tamim. Walls surrounded this part of the Old City, but five centuries ago the City expanded beyond the walls and no new walls were built, because there was no need for them. Nevertheless, the architectural style and the urban fabric are similar inside and outside the walls. Naturally, though, the part inside the walls that you see in front of you in the model is older.

I feel that I'm looking at the Old City from an airplane. I'm positioned above it, and can see it with all its details... houses, quarters, different buildings, and its spectacular Citadel. Oh my father, I remember the aerial-view photograph I found among your papers!

Isn't this an attractive sight to see from here, Tamim? How do you find our tour today?

It is wonderful, Dad. All the tours were great. Thanks Dad.

Let's get back.

*   *   *

They got back to where Tamim's father had parked his car. On their way back, Tamim did not stop asking questions, one after another, and his father's replies were sometimes satisfactory, other times incomplete or postponed, because some answers are more useful when backed up by documents, maps, or actual visits to the site.

5

Visiting *al-Jdayde* Quarter

An alleyway in al-Jdayde Quarter

One weekend morning, Tamim came to his father carrying a sketchbook in his hand. His father was sitting at his desk, writing down his notes and filing some of his papers.

Look what I've drawn, Dad.

Let's see what you have. Show me.

Tamim opened his sketchbook to a certain page, put it in front of his father, and said:

Have a look.

The father looked at the page in the sketchbook. He was surprised to see a drawing of an alley in old Aleppo.

Did you draw this yourself?

Yes, Dad. Didn't you tell me to draw what I see and put it on paper?

That's right.

That's exactly what I did.

How did that happen, Tamim? When did

you go to the Old City? Did you go there by yourself? This is a beautiful drawing, indeed. Where and when did you draw it?

Well, Dad. First, let me tell you what happened. I talked to my friend, Fadi, in school about our visit to the Citadel, to *Souk al-Medina* and to other quarters in the Old City. He liked what he heard and asked if we could take him with us on our next visit there. By the way, when and where is our next visit going to be?

My questions to you go unanswered. Instead, I get two questions from you. Listen, Tamim. When and where did you draw this?

Just wait a minute, Dad. Your questions will be answered if you let me tell you the rest of the story. Fadi told me that he lives in a neighborhood not too far from the Old City, and from time to time, he and his parents visit his grandmother, who lives in a beautiful house in one of the quarters of the Old City called *al-Jdayde.*

Kamal responded, trying to show Tamim his surprise and disapproval:

So you went to *al-Jdayde* Quarter and visited Fadi's grandmother in her beautiful house, and...

Yes, Dad. On my way back, I took out my sketchbook and started drawing this picture that I liked. Look, Dad, what is your opinion? How do you find my drawing? What do you think about this protruding wooden room in the first floor? It's a room overlooking the quarter from Fadi's grandma's house.

Beautiful, Tamim, but what did you leave for our joint visit to *al-Jdayde*? Have you seen everything there? I was planning on going there with you on our next sightseeing tour.

No, Dad. I'm still looking forward to going there with you. A visit with you has a different flavor. I enjoy your explanation and like all the information you give me.

After a careful examination of the drawing, his father said:

Let's get back to the drawing, Tamim. People of Aleppo call this wooden room overlooking the quarter from Fadi's grandmother's house a *kishk*. It is the Aleppian house's first opening to the quarter outside. Such houses have been always closed to the outside; instead, they open to a courtyard from the inside, providing gentle, cool weather and privacy for the people who live there.

Looking further at the drawing he continued:

I see that your lines are strong, and so is your observation. Do you agree with me, though, that this line would be better if tilted this way? Also, look at these two lines: they must be vertical in real life, so make them vertical in your drawing.

Tamim's father continued making comments on the drawing to his son, and gave him a simplified idea about drawing architectural perspectives. Tamim simply accepted his father's comments and started asking him about other things related to the drawing. The dialogue between them ended with a good impression for both. On one hand, Kamal discovered his son's interest in the Old City, an interest that led him to talk about it to his friends. He also found that his son had an ability to express what he saw in drawing, and that his strong lines were impressive and quite telling of a potential talent.

On the other hand, Tamim was pleased for two reasons. First, he did not get a lecture

A kishk in al-Jdayde neighborhood before and after restoration

The Emergence of Suburbs Outside the Old City Walls
Al-Jdayde Quarter as an Example

Toward the beginning of the fifteenth century, the Tartar armies of Tamerlane invaded Aleppo, destroying and burning much of it. Many of its inhabitant, including Christians, fled the city temporarily. They later returned to repair their houses and resume their lives. They built new houses outside the city walls. Thus, new quarters emerged. In time, those quarters expanded to become suburbs for the Old City. In the '80s of the twentieth century, the two remaining eastern and northern suburbs were registered as a part of the Old City, in a special decision issued by the Ministry of Culture.

In the fifteenth century, Christians chose for themselves the northwestern corner of the city for their expansion. Al-Jdayde Quarter (al-Jadeeda, Arabic for "new," or al-Judayda, the diminutive form of the word) was built, modeled on the quarters of the city inside the walls. Churches and monasteries were built as well. There were also houses of different sizes such as Ghazale, Achaqbash, Baseel, and Wakeel houses, which are among the largest and greatest ones. The splendor and magnificence of these houses reflected the affluence of their owners and those who worked in trade in Aleppo at the time.

Aleppo, which has been an important trading center throughout different eras, was also a temporary stop for Armenians (as Christians coming from the Northeast) on their way to the Holy City of Jerusalem. Traveling pilgrims gathered to visit the holy places in Palestine. For this purpose, Aleppo was a restful shelter from the long tiring journey. Thus, in time, they built an inn or "khan" outside the walls (today it is known as al-Hukidon, the Armenian word for the Spiritual House) to stay for several days before they resumed their journey to Jerusalem.

Armenian relations with Aleppo were strengthened, especially in the thirteenth century. Aleppo became a residence for many Armenians, whose numbers increased over time. Furthermore, other Armenians came from Persia (Iran today) and started working in trade and industry in Aleppo, making good fortunes. They settled in the city and built themselves what they needed in terms of houses and churches. Among their most significant and oldest churches in al-Jdayde Quarter is the "Church of the Forty Martyrs," one of the oldest Churches in this quarter of Old Aleppo. It was built on the site of a small temple inside an old cemetery about the year of 1440. The temple was expanded and converted into a church more than once. The most significant expansion was in 1499. Then it was expanded once again in 1616 during the Ottoman Period. It became a large Church raised on columns and piers and roofed by arches and vaults, attaining the plan of the typical church and becoming a magnificent structure. In 1869, the Church underwent restoration works, and then more restoration took place in the '50s of the twentieth century.

It has an underground floor carved in the bedrock that carries it. This floor can be accessed by a staircase carved in the same rock, which leads to two facing vaulted halls (iwan). This place might have been used before the Church was established.

The Church was named after the Forty Martyrs who had been killed by the pagan Romans in the nearby Armenian city of "Siwas."

The bell tower of the Forty Martyrs Armenian Church in Jdayde Quarter

The cave under the Forty Martyrs Armenian Church

from his father for his "adventure" in the Old City with his friend Fadi. Second, his father liked his drawing. He corrected some lines and gave him advice to improve his drawing. Tamim immediately corrected the drawing. Now, he found it more acceptable than before.

*   *   *

On the next day, Kamal took his son on a tour in the *al-Jdayde* Quarter. They entered it through one of the busy commercial centers that led to it and branched off from *al-Khandaq* (Trench) Street.

Dad, why is this wide street called "*al-Khandaq* Street," and where is the trench the street was named after?

This street forms the barrier between the Old City inside the walls and its northern suburbs outside the walls. At the beginning of the fifteenth century, the Old City expanded outside its walls, here. It was surrounded by the walls that protected it. Gates that led to the city were distributed along these walls. For instance, the walls here were extending form *Bab al-Hadid* in the east to *Bab al-Nasr*, and ending in the west with *Bab al-Faraj*,

Decorated window in Ibshir Pasha Endowment in Jdayde Quarter

which crumbled and has disappeared now. The trench is the area behind the walls extending northward. This area is lower than the walls in order to increase their height and to make it harder to climb up the walls or break into the city.

So the trench disappeared!

Yes, and the walls too. They are no longer needed to protect the city. So this street, which connects the east of Aleppo with its west, was constructed and called *al-Khandaq* Street because it was built on the location of the trench behind the walls.

They walked together along the commercial hub that led them to the quarter. They saw different shops with a wide variety of merchandise. After that, they stopped at an intersection.

Those people over there sell sweets, and those to the right sell chicken. That market sells all kinds of fish: river fish as well as sea fish. The street on the left through this arch, however, is specialized for selling the wool that women use for knitting clothes. But in that street to the far left, vendors are specialized in selling women coats and...

So, *al-Jdayde* quarter is a commercial area!

No, we're only in one part of it, Tamim. Come this way, we're going to *Sahet al-Hatab* (the Firewood Square).

What is "*Sahet al-Hatab*"?

It is that wide open area where a number of streets and alleys meet. In the past, firewood was brought here to be sold to people. Firewood is that dry wood chopped from tree trunks and branches to be used in houses, where it is burnt in fireplaces or in stoves for cooking and heating. Oil products were not yet known at that time.

They reached *Sahet al-Hatab*. Tamim liked the open space with high trees and benches all around it where people could sit to take a rest, or someone could spend time talking to a friend or watching his kids play in a safe place.

Come this way Tamim... I'll show you something important.

What is it, Dad?

A few years ago, this square was not in the same condition as it is today. It was full of random buildings added to the original ones, distorting the character of this space and causing noise. But they were removed, and the space is back to its original condition as the square you see today.

By the way, look, Tamim, this mosque was built in *Sahet al-Hatab* at the beginning of the sixteenth century and called Sharaf Mosque. The street it's on goes all the way to a famous shopping street called *al-Tilal* Street.

Sahet al-Hatab in Jdayde Quarter

Right, Dad, I know it. Years ago I went there with my mother a few times. I remember its name.

Pointing to another corner of the quarter, Tamim's father said:

A narrow alley branches off from this corner of the square, leading to another square we'll visit later. Come, now, let's take this alley.

As they went through that narrow alley, Tamim noticed that it had shops only on the right side. Those shops specialized in selling ladies' bags. On the opposite side, however, there was a high wall, almost three stories high. Many other alleys branched off from there, and they entered the first one. Kamal said to his son:

This is a residential alley, Tamim. That's why you see doors of houses all the way, until the end of the alley.

I think Fadi's grandma's house is in this alley! I can see the protruding wooden room '*al kishk*' over there. I think that Fadi is waiting for us there because I told him that we'd go to visit al-Jdayde Quarter today.

It is quite possible that the house is not in this alley; it may be in the next one or the one after... These alleys look the same, and all of them have wooden kishks, so the person who visits this alley for only one time could be confused. Come now, let's enter this house.

Tamim saw a sign on the house saying "House," and in smaller letters on the same sign it had the words "Hotel, Restaurant." Tamim asked his father:

Metal covered door with pattern made up of nail heads

How can this place be a house, a hotel, and a restaurant, all at the same time?

It was a house, but it had been abandoned for a long time, until its owners decided to convert it to a hotel and restaurant — some sort of investment in tourism, which I believe is a good idea.

When they entered the house, they found themselves in a small space open in many directions. They entered through a small door into a high spacious hall that had many spaces; the middle one was the highest and was covered with a beautiful dome.

A receptionist welcomed them. Kamal asked her about his friend the director of the place; she answered that he was abroad, and added:

Is there anything I can help you with?

Thank you. Can we have a look at this beautiful house? This is my son, Tamim. He wants to see the house. I hope that doesn't cause any inconvenience. We'll just stand here in the courtyard.

You are quite welcome. Most guests are out now. Why don't you proceed to the left and take your time. You can visit all the spaces, and you'll find someone to assist you.

As they went through another small door,

Main reception hall of house converted to hotel in Jdayde Quarter. Walls are missing their wooden paneling

its own bathroom and other amenities.

The atmosphere is quite nice here, Dad! The air is absolutely healthy and fresh. It's very quiet in here, too. But still, the most beautiful thing is the lush green color of the shrubs and the colorful flowers, which make the place wonderful.

Come, let's visit the other part of the house, Tamim. Before we do so, let me tell you something about this hall.

They came back to the reception hall again. Kamal started telling

they found themselves in a spacious courtyard surrounded by rooms. There was a staircase leading to the first floor, where there were other rooms overlooking that courtyard.

This part of the house became a hotel, Tamim, and those rooms are accommodations for the guests. Each room has

the story of the wooden panels that covered the walls of the hall.

At the beginning of the twentieth century, this house was abandoned. While residing in Aleppo at the time, a wealthy German lady who was interested in artifacts and cultures paid it a visit. She admired its hall and the wooden paneling on the walls with their beautiful and

Wooden paneling of house on facing page is exhibited as the "Aleppo Room" at the Berlin Museum

time, after hearing about it from the German lady. It is believed that he did not see the paneling in its original location, but sent someone on his behalf and offered to purchase it from the house owners. They agreed to sell it for a certain amount of Ottoman gold currency, and the decorative paneling was transported in wooden crates to Germany. After almost thirty years, during which time parts of the paneling were damaged and restored, it was put on display in the museum of Berlin in 1960. The paneling was installed in a special area in the museum and set up the same way as its original arrangement in this ancient Aleppian house. It became one of the museum's important displays and was called "The Aleppian Room."

colorful drawings. The drawings were distributed in rhythm with the pattern of openings, whether windows or cupboards, and each cladding panel had a calligraphic plate above it featuring a line of poetry, an aphorism, or a proverb.

The director of the Islamic Arts Museum in Berlin was interested in this wooden paneling when he visited Aleppo at that

This is a lovely story, but it would have been lovelier to have the wooden paneling here in its location cladding the walls of this hall, because I can't imagine these walls in any other way.

Remind me to show you a book about this room in my office, later today, Tamim.

Are there any pictures of the panels of the wooden cladding in the book?

Yes, Tamim. It contains detailed descriptions and pictures of that paneling. By the way, the book is based on a German researcher's doctoral dissertation in the field of "History of Art." It was translated into Arabic years ago. In addition, this room was later the focus of much research on the wooden claddings in ancient Aleppian houses. Some researchers studied the proverbs and verses that were written on them, while others studied the drawing and coloring techniques and things like that.

They returned to the small entrance lobby, where they went through another door.

Come this way, Tamim, we'll go to the other part of the house, which has been turned into a restaurant.

They walked through a narrow corridor into a room, and from there, they went into the courtyard of this section of the house. Tamim marveled at its beauty. The green trees were like a canopy covering the courtyard. They walked through aisles of restaurant tables and chairs, then turned back to have a look at the spectacular *iwan*, moving

The main courtyard of house converted to a restaurant at Jdayde Quarter

their eyes around to enjoy the ornaments on the facades overlooking the courtyard and its central pond. There was a fountain in the middle of the pond and a high platform behind it.

What's this high area behind the pond, Dad?

It's the musicians' *mastaba*. It is found in a number of luxurious ancient Aleppian houses. The owner of the house built it in this location as a place for singers and musicians to sit and entertain the house owners and their guests with their performances.

Are those evening parties still held? Can we attend one of them?

Those evening parties are not as common nowadays as they were in the past, but I'll try to see when one of them will be held, at a house of a friend or an acquaintance, and will take you with me. Now, come this way.

They stood near the door where they had entered the courtyard, and went through an adjacent door that led to a descending staircase. After that, they found themselves in a low space roofed by a vaulted ceiling.

This basement was used by the house owners for storing the supplies they needed year round, Tamim.

I think it is now used as a part of the restaurant upstairs.

That's right, Tamim. Now come, let's take these stairs down.

They went down another set of stairs, until they found themselves in a cave!

Where are we now, Dad?

We're now in a natural cave of limestone, found underneath this house. It is obvious that the previous tenants also used it for storage. They dug and carved additional parts in the rocks for use, like these stairs and those spaces over there.

That's amazing, Dad! Are there similar caves in other houses as well?

There are caves found in the bedrock under many houses in *al-Jdayde* and other quarters, but most of them are now filled up with earth and closed, because they are no longer needed under houses these days.

They went back up from the cave to the basement and then to the beautiful courtyard. Amazement was clearly visible on Tamim's face. His father thanked the restaurant manager. Finally, they returned to the hall to thank the receptionist and ask her to give Kamal's best regards to his traveling friend. After that, they left the place.

What do you think about this visit, Tamim?

Wonderful, Dad! It's a grand and luxurious Aleppian house, indeed.

There are many houses like this one in

A traditional musical performance at a Jdayde house

this area, as well as in other areas such as *al-Farafra* and *Bab Qinnisreen*.

They walked up the alley, taking the same route they had taken to get there. Tamim asked his father about a remark he had made earlier when they entered that house.

You said that by turning the house into a hotel and restaurant, the house owners did the right thing. What do you mean by that?

Well, to be precise, the house belongs now to the descendants of the original owners. They are the new owners who did this project. And they did the right thing because the way we live today has changed so much since the old days. These large houses are no longer fit as residential accommodations for a modern Aleppian family. Putting a house that had been abandoned for a long time back into use as a hotel or a restaurant has two benefits. First, it helps in repairing, restoring, and refurbishing the house for that proper investment. Therefore, the house is saved from deterioration and collapse due to abandonment. Second, the new use provides constant maintenance for such large houses, although this may have its own hazards.

Thanks, Dad. What you say sounds reasonable.

Come now. Before we leave the alley, we'll go into another house, which has just been converted into a restaurant.

They went through a door that led them into the corner of a vast space, a courtyard furnished with tables and chairs. Another receptionist welcomed them. Going through the courtyard, they descended to the vault and took a quick look at the cave of the house. Then they climbed back up to the courtyard. Before leaving, they thanked the person who had welcomed them, who invited them to come back again.

After getting back through the alley to the Firewood Square, Tamim asked:

Have many houses in this area been turned into a tourism investment?

Yes, Tamim. This trend gives the area a new appeal for tourists, and turns old houses into commercial investments.

But you said there are still residential houses in the quarter.

That's right, Tamim. This is a residential quarter, but there are some commercial centers too, since changing the use of these houses from a residential use to a touristic one did not include medium-size and small houses. Those are still inhabited by their owners and residents.

Like Fadi's grandma's house, and others like it. Am I right?

Yes, Tamim. By the way, I think according to your description that Fadi's grandmother's house must be in the next alley, parallel to this one. Come. Let's go there.

I hope that Fadi is still waiting.

I hope so, because I admired your friend through what you said about him, and

Fadi, Tamim, and his father during their visit to Jdayde Quarter

because you like him, too.

They entered the gate of the next alley and walked straight ahead. Meanwhile, Kamal kept talking to his son about the change of use of some houses they were walking past:

This large house was also converted into a hotel, and that one into a restaurant, while this one here on our right, which is the grandest and oldest, was converted into an institute for training young men to be tourist guides or to work in the field of hotel and hospitality services.

They reached a house that had a beautiful kishk above its entrance.

Isn't this Fadi's grandmother's house? This looks like the kishk overlooking the alley that you drew.

That's right, Dad. Let me knock on the door.

Tamim tried to raise his body, standing on the tips of his toes. He took hold of the little metal door knocker, which was in the shape of a hand, and knocked on the door twice. The door was opened and Fadi appeared with his small head poking out of the door. He said:

Welcome, come in. How are you, Uncle?

Hello, Fadi. I'm fine, and you?

Fine, thank you. I have a surprise for you today. My father is here visiting my grandmother and he would like to get to know you.

Tamim and his father entered a small space,

In grandmother's house, Fadi and Tamim talking through a courtyard window

Fadi's grandmother knitting under a jasmine tree

This is my father, Dr. Wadie, and this is Tamim's father, Mr Kamal, the father of my friend Tamim, whom I told you about many times.

You told me about him and his father. You are welcome, I'm glad to meet you. You are welcome!

Pleased to meet you, too.

In the courtyard, Tamim swiveled his eyes around, trying to see everything in the space, which had a pond in its center and a citron tree with some fruits. There was a jasmine tree with beautiful, sweet-smelling white flowers in the corner of the courtyard, opposite and near the stairs that led to the first floor. Fadi's father started out by saying:

This is the family house, where my brothers and I were born and grew up. However, I'm living now in *al-Aziziya* Quarter, close to my office, and only my mother still lives here now.

and then they moved to the open courtyard of the house, where they saw an elegantly dressed man, about forty years old, wearing thin, fine glasses without a frame. Fadi introduced him to them, saying:

He pointed in the direction of a dignified old lady wearing glasses perched on the top of her nose, sitting in a side of the courtyard and knitting wool to make a woolen jacket.

Hello, ma'am, how are you?

Welcome, son. I'm OK, thank God. Thank you.

How's your house? Are you happy living here?

I am used to living in it. I don't move around much, but I do spend most of my time here. My son Abu Fadi and my grandson Fadi visit me from time to time and provide me with everything I need. Fadi sometimes visits me and stays with me for a night or two. My son often invites me to visit him and stay at his place, but I prefer my house.

Fadi invited me to meet you and to visit your house.

You are welcome.

Fadi's father said:

This house is neither big nor luxurious, Abu Tamim. It is of a moderate size, and most of the houses here are of the same size or even smaller.

It is beautiful, but having you here makes it more beautiful. I think that it contains most of the necessary architectural elements for decent living.

Right, its only defect may be the difficulty of moving between its rooms and spaces in winter, passing through the courtyard when the weather is very cold. For this reason we protect ourselves by wearing an extra woolen jacket while moving around, and my mother still does so.

Meanwhile, Fadi was in the kitchen preparing something that his grandmother would usually present to her guests. He came back

A Jdayde house courtyard with two sets of stairs, one leading to the first floor, the other leading to the roof

carrying a tray that contained small dishes with a piece of yellow fruit in each of them.

Have some of it, Uncle. This is citron jam, which my grandmother made.

Fadi's father added:

It is from that tree, there. My mother makes this jam from its fruit.

Tamim and his father tasted some of the jam.

Tamim said:

Oh my God! How delicious! Isn't it, Dad?

It is delicious, indeed! Thank you, Um Wadie. This is very kind of you.

The courtyard of a large Jdayde house with a fountain and a musicians' mastaba

I'm glad you liked it. God bless you.

All of them stood in the courtyard next to Fadi's grandmother. They got more acquainted with each other and exchanged conversation about different subjects, and then they wandered around the house. Meanwhile, Fadi was talking proudly and happily to his friend, Tamim, about some of the specific details of his grandmother's house.

Finally, you came to my grandmother's house and saw this old Aleppian house that I like!

Fadi took Tamim by the arm, and they moved away, whispering to each other. When they rejoined the group, Tamim said to his father:

When are we going to visit the Old City, and where are we going to go this time, Father? Fadi would like to come with us.

He is welcome. When we decide on the time, we'll tell him. You're also invited, Abu Fadi.

Thank you, brother, it would be my pleasure. I will go with you if the time is suitable for me. Thank you.

After saying good-bye, Tamim and his father left Fadi's grandmother's house, with their best regards and good wishes for them.

*   *   *

They went back the *zouqaq* that branched off from the alley with the high wall on its left side. Then they walked westward to arrive at a somewhat large square with a statue of a man seated on a chair in its center. Tamim asked:

An infrastructure renovation and repair construction site

Who does this statue represent, Dad?

It represents one of the greatest Christian clergymen of more than two centuries ago. That church behind him belongs to the denomination he headed, and in front is a square named after him. Look, on this side there is a church for another denomination, and there is a road here that leads to a third church, a fourth, and so on.

This area looks like a cluster of churches.

Yes, Tamim, actually it is. We will visit some of these churches the next time.

The road that branches off from this square seems to be closed. I see construction going on, Dad. What are they doing?

Yes, it is under construction, and this is not the only site where something like this is being carried out. We saw such work in other locations we visited. Do you remember? These construction works are aimed at repairing and renovating the infrastructure.

What do you mean by "infrastructure," Dad?

A complex group of networks and ditches is usually constructed in cities underneath their streets, roads, and allies. Some of them bring water from water purification plants to supply houses and buildings; others carry drainage water called "sewage," which comes from houses and other places, to run through pipes to be drained far away from the city. In addition, there are phone and electricity networks that serve buildings located on the sides of streets and alleys.

How was the city before these works?

There were problems with the drainage of water. Nearly one hundred years ago a network for sewage was built, but over time, it became damaged and crumbled, and its water started to leak underground, affecting the foundations of buildings. So the department of the Old City and its rehabilitation project gave priority to the restoration and renovation process, involving all kinds of those net-

works. Thus, many infrastructure projects have been carried out here and there as needed.

Now look, Tamim, what do you see on the top of this alley?

I see an arch carrying a structure, like a room with two windows above the alley. It is a nice scene. Can we pass under it?

Of course, but only after the project of repairing and repaving the alley is completed. We will do this when we visit other houses and sites in this area, going through under this *sibat*.

What is "*sibat*," Dad?

It is that structure above the alley, carried by that arch. *Sibat* is a distinctive Aleppian architectural feature that gives beauty to the alley, covering part of it and providing shade and protection to pedestrians passing under it.

I remember seeing something like this sibat when we visited a quarter inside *Bab Qinnisreen*.

Excellent, Tamim. The sibat is quite common all around the Old City, inside and outside the walls.

On their way back, Tamim kept asking about sites and other matters, and his father calmly answered him, satisfy his curiosity and desire to know everything during that visit and in the Old City as a whole.

Alleyway passages under "sibats" in typical Jdayde neighborhoods

6

A Visit to an
Old Aleppian House

A residential neighborhood in the Old City of Aleppo

Accompanied by Fadi, Tamim and his father drove to the Old City in their car, as Tamim's father had promised. It was a nice spring day. The sky was clear after it had rained heavily for the past few days. It had stopped raining just the evening before.

Where are we going today, Dad?

We are going to visit an old house of a friend of mine.

Before arriving at their destination, Tamim shouted as if he had discovered something:

Aren't we going to *Bab Qinnisreen?* That's the beautiful gate over there at the end of the street.

Right, Tamim. You've got a sharp memory.

Here Fadi said:

Tamim already told me about this place, didn't he?

That's right, Fadi. Look! The wall of the City is on your left, and that high ground on your right is *Tallet as-Sawda* (the Black Hill). Here we are now. Look! That is *Bab Qinnisreen.*

This time, Tamim turned into a guide, presenting information to his friend and feeling proud of what he knew. He felt ecstatic when Fadi asked him a question and he could answer it right away. He glanced at his father's eyes, in case he was giving the wrong information, but his father ignored such glances; he did not want to correct his son. He let Tamim feel free to tell his friend what he knew. If he did make a mistake, he would be corrected at home, rather than in front of his friend. That is, unless his mistake was serious!

Tamim started explaining to his friend:

Look at this gate. It's where people used to come into the city during the daytime, but it's closed with this huge door at night. Moreover, look at these small and narrow slots in the walls. They were used for defending the gate and shooting arrows at the enemies outside the walls when the city was under siege.

Door with metal ring used as door-knocker

He continued explaining as they toured every point and site. Fadi was surprised by what he saw and heard, especially that his friend, Tamim, knew so much more than Fadi did. Tamim knew more details, even though they were together in the same grade at school.

They all walked into the main center of the quarter, but a few minutes later they turned right, then left, then right once again. Tamim's father interrupted the conversation and explanations:

 We are here, boys.

They all stood in front of a door that seemed to be covered with tin. It was painted black, with protruding iron nails hammered into its face. These nails were arranged skillfully to form a pattern, with an attractive and beautiful design. Above the middle of the door, there was a small handle, shaped like a hand holding a little ball. This was made of cast iron, with fine details.

Where are we now, Dad? Didn't you say we were going to visit an old house in Aleppo?

Yes, Tamim. Here we are in the alley, and that is the house of my friend, Abu Wael. But before we get into the house, look at its construction from outside. What can you see?

What can we see? We see a high, blank wall with no openings. Its looks ordinary, compared to some of what we've seen in our earlier visits to the Old City, such as

Tamim and Fadi closing the door after entering Abu Wael's house

the facade of a khan or the entrance of an old hammam or a palace. Dad, at first sight, I can see that this alley is like those of Al-Jdayde Quarter, which we visited earlier.

Iwan in an Aleppian house with patterned flooring of colored marble

 Tamim, this facade, like those of the neighboring houses, hides unexpected beauty inside.

Tamim's father gripped the hanging hand on the door's panel, pulled it, and then let it go. All of them heard a loud knock on the door. Tamim smiled to his friend, and his father gripped the hand once again and started knocking on the door as if he was playing a rhythmic tune.

They heard a voice from inside the house asking: Who is it?

 Open the door, Abu Wael. It's me, Abu Tamim.

They heard the sound of a latch being pulled. The door opened, and Wael's father appeared, smiling and greeting them:

 Just in time, as always, Abu Tamim. Come in, you are welcome.

They entered the house and found themselves in a small entrance with a low ceiling. Wael's father walked in front of them, and then turned left, where they found themselves in an open courtyard. Almost in the center was a masonry pond with a fountain, and water flowing from its top. The sound of the cascading water broke the silence of the place.

Tamim looked around. He noticed that the upper facades were decorated. One of them was built in the *Ablaq* style. He saw an interior space inside the building, above which was a masonry arch with an engraved front. He also saw trees with green leaves and orange and yellow fruit.

Tamim shook his head as if he was trying to wake up from his amazement, and looked at his friend Fadi, then at his father, as if seeking an explanation from the former:

Did you see what I saw, Fadi?

Or, as if asking his father, while overwhelmed:

What is this, Dad? How beautiful your friend's house is!

Tamim's father interrupted the boys' train of thought, making an introduction:

This is my friend, Omar, or Abu Wael, and this is his house. This is my son, Tamim, and that is his friend, Fadi.

Your house is beautiful, Uncle Abu Wael.

Abu Wael, we have come to visit you, as I told you two days ago, in order to give these two youngsters a chance to know you and to show them around your house.

You are all welcome. Have you visited any houses in the Old City yet?

Fadi answered him, saying:

My grandmother's house is in the *al-Jdayde* quarter. But apparently it is smaller than yours. There are no decorations in it, and its pool is smaller, and there is only one tree. Tamim and his father and I visited it a few days ago.

Wael's father said:

This one was my grandfather's house, and I was born here. My children were born in the hospital, but they were brought up in this house before they got married and went to live in the modern part of the city.

Show us your house in detail. The boys are eager to know more about it.

This vast space inside the building with a vaulted ceiling, as you see, is *al-iwan*, or as the Aleppian people say, *al-liwan*. In Aleppo, it always faces the north. It is where the family sits, shaded from

Painted wooden wall paneling in the "Aleppo Room"

the sunlight in summer. It also protects them against the strong wind and the cold in other seasons. It enables them to see the beauty of the courtyard with its pond, its trees, and its open space.

Wael's father walked ahead, and asked the group to follow him:

This way, please.

He went onto the floor of the iwan, followed by the group. Tamim turned and saw the view of the courtyard from within the iwan. He smiled and looked into Fadi's eyes, which expressed amazement.

As if he wanted to continue comparing this house with his grandmother's, Fadi said:

In my grandmother's house, there is no such space like this *liwan*. (Looking up, he continued:) It is quite beautiful, this space!

Then Wael's father walked through a door on one of the two facing walls of the iwan, and the group followed him. They found themselves in a large room: its walls were covered with wooden panels, with some colored paintings on them. The ceiling was covered and painted in same manner.

Tamim was amazed at what he saw. He gazed at his friend, as if asking him: "What do you think, Fadi? Don't t tell me there is a room like this one in your grandmother's house!" But he remained silent and continued looking at the paintings and colors, and then asked Wael's father:

Aren't these lines of writing above the windows?

You are right, Tamim. These are verses of rhymed Arabic poetry, chosen from a famous poem, most of which express human aphorisms and experiences.

Tamim's father said:

Your room needs much more care. You have to start repairing it.

You are right, but I am afraid I might not find someone who could repair it properly.

Maybe I will find somebody to restore it for you. But do you agree with me that this room is over two hundred years old?

Here Tamim asked his father:

Father, you mentioned the word "restore" once again. What is the meaning of "restore"?

Don't worry, I'll explain that all later.

According to my study of the history of this house, I think that it is over two hundred and fifty years old, judging by other similar rooms with wooden panels at different sites. (Turning to the boys:) Look now, guys: the wall of this room from inside overlooks the courtyard through these windows. Facing them on the opposite, interior wall were the same number of built-in deep cupboards.

How do the cupboards exist in the walls?

They are parts of the original construction.

He opened the two wooden shutters of one of the cupboards, to show the boys how its depth equaled the thickness of the wall.

Why is the wall so thick?

Tamim's father answered:

The walls are thick here, Tamim, because they were the main parts of the building construction in the past. They bore the ceilings and often had another story above them. Moreover, thick walls have a significant advantage, for they provide the necessary insulation. They are called *al-kalean*. As you see, the cupboard is deep, and it is used for storing things. This one contains some of Abu Wael's books, so it is called a "bookcase."

What does insulation mean, father?

It is the process of separating two mediums or spaces from each other. This way, if the weather outside is cold, it will not make the rooms cold, because of the thickness of the walls; the weather inside the rooms will be mild. Similarly, in summer, when it is very hot outside, the walls

A small Kishk (mashrabiyya) overlooking the alleyway

will act as an insulator from the heat.

Of course, this reduces the expenses of heating. Moreover, we are not in need of air-conditioning.

By the way, is there any *badhindge* in your house, Abu Wael?

Wael's father walked towards the end of the room, pointed at a hole over the cupboard before the last one, and said:

Look at that covered hole up there. It is a natural air-conditioner (*badhindge*).

What does "*badhindge*" mean, Uncle Abu Wael?

It is a Persian word, Tamim. In Arabic, it means the "air catcher." It is a vertical shaft, or a void fitted in the thick walls of the building (*al-kalean*). It begins here from this room with this opening, goes up to the roof of the house, and ends up in another opening. Certainly, in Aleppo, the opening on the roof faces the west, where air comes clean in the summer, carried by the wind from the seaside.

In practical terms, the air enters into the roof opening and goes down through the shaft inside the wall, until it reaches us here. This way, it softens the hot atmosphere in the room.

This is a simple and easy form of air-conditioning, bringing in the cold air in summer. A piece of wet canvas may also be placed at the end of the vertical canal and next to the opening inside the wall over there (pointing at the hole of the *badhindge*). This piece of canvas is dampened every now and then to make the air moist and fresh.

So, this is a primitive way of air-conditioning.

That's right, Tamim. Let us call it a natural way instead, as it is not costly, except for the expenses of establishing it in the thick wall, and making its two openings, down here and up on the roof. There is also no additional electricity expenditure, nor air-conditioning equipment maintenance cost. I love this room more than I love the others. It is where I receive my guests; its walls please my eyes with its wooden decorated panels; the paintings on its walls are colored and beautiful; my books and things that I love are inside its cupboards.

The carved masonry decorations of a house in Aleppo, now used as an elementary school

Before leaving the room, they went down to a lower level. Tamim noticed that the low floor was decorated with colored stone tiling. He wanted to attract Fadi's attention, but instead he said to his father:

Father, look at this beautiful floor. It looks like a colored carpet.

You're right, Tamim. This is the threshold of the room. We call it *al-atabe*. It is usually lower than the level of the floor of the room itself. The lower section is where the family and the guests take off their shoes before stepping onto the higher

THE OLD ALEPPIAN HOUSES

The old Aleppian house with its inner courtyard is an ideal historic form of residence. It spread in the ancient Middle East thousands of years ago, and was an advanced state of housing cell, providing safety and stability for its inhabitants, averting mother nature's danger and its alternating climate, and providing its inhabitants with familial gatherings and social bonding. For this, it is the most suitable and appropriate climatically, and most responsive to Middle Eastern cultures and oriental traditions, including the requirements for privacy and independence.

The Aleppo house, along with its components, wasn't built all at once, nor was it built according to a fixed plan. Rather, it was built in stages according to the residents' needs and priorities.

The inner courtyard is the essence of the architectural design concept of the house, and the center of family life takes place within it. It is also the core of the house, from which all the spaces and rooms branch out. The facades surrounding the courtyard have a particular importance. Often, they were quite beautiful—adorned and decorated with carved patterns. By contrast, the external wall facades overlooking the alley were sullen and had few openings. This contrast between the beauty inside and the austerity outside causes an unexpected feeling of bewilder-

The kishk of a residence overlooks a typical Aleppo alleyway

ment when strangers enter into an old house in Aleppo.

The evergreen of the planted trees in the courtyard (usually citrus trees), along with the pond and the sound of water cascading from its fountain, add charm and appeal to the house.

*   *   *

The old Aleppian house is built using hard limestone, which is available in the quarries near Aleppo. This gives its construction strength, firmness, and durability. The construction method of the thick walls (al-kalean) contributes to the strength and insulation of the structure. At the beginning, the ceilings were made as vaults (continuous or crossing vaults over the complete space area). Later on, timber beams, from the long and straight trunks of fir trees, were used.

*   *   *

The old Aleppian house consists of a group of spaces: their size and number depend on the wealth of its owner. These spaces also affect the luxury of the building, its finishes and accessories, and the richness of the adornment and decoration.

Perhaps the most important part of the house is the "iwan," but this is not found in every house. This space has one side that is open and overlooking the courtyard, and always oriented towards the north in Aleppo. Its facade often has a carved and adorned arch with a high ceiling. This "iwan" provides the residents of the house with a peaceful and relaxed sitting area during the hot summer days. Its floor is at a higher level than the courtyard, and its large volume and configuration dominates the courtyard and its contents, as well as the rest of the indoor facades of the house.

Some rich Aleppian houses may contain an unusual space, larger than the rest of the rooms, called al-qa'a (the hall). This space is often over two stories high, and covered with a dome. Its facade overlooks the courtyard, and this is where the owners welcome their visitors. Its floor and walls are usually covered with rich and luxurious materials. The wooden cladding on the walls pleasantly harmonizes with the window openings and the in-wall cupboards of the room. It is a domain to showcase fine artistry and craftsmanship in drawing, calligraphy, and attractive colors. The flooring is tiled with colored marble and stone pieces that form exquisite geometric ornaments. The qa'a may have a small pond in its center, built and decorated with colorful stones.

The Aleppian houses are compact residential cells reached through alleys and lanes, forming in its total "the residential neighborhood," which can also include a number of public buildings such as schools, worship houses, public bath (hammam), shops, etc. The neighborhood groups form that unique traditional urban fabric of Old Aleppo.

Architectural features of Aleppo houses include iwan, qa'a (hall), and dome

A fountain inside the qa'a of a house in Aleppo, surrounded by geometric floor tiling

level, usually covered with carpets.

You're right, Kamal. If you had visited us a week ago, we would have asked you —kindly— to take off your shoes before stepping into the room where the carpets were laid on the floors during winter.

This beautiful floor down here is tiled with colored flagstones, some of which are marble, designed in a specific geometrical and decorative way. This kind of decoration is called "masonry mosaic."

Didn't we see geometrical decorations like these on the floor of the iwan?

Yes, your observation is correct, but there is a difference between the two in the geometrical and decorative design.

They all went out of the room to the courtyard. Within moments, a lady approached them, holding a tray on which there were glasses of yellow juice. She started talking to Tamim's father:

Welcome, Abu Tamim. How are you? How is Um Tamim? She is not with you today!

Thanks Um Wael. How are you, too? How are the children? Are they OK? Um Tamim says hello to you. As you know, she is busy at home in the morning. We have come today to visit you. These two boys would like to see your beautiful house.

Welcome. Please help yourselves.

She served juice to the group, and Kamal took a glass and said:

This is a sweetened lemon juice, isn't it?

Wael's father said:

This juice is made from the lemons of that tree over there (pointing at a green, high, and leafy tree). There are still some lemons up there waiting to be picked.

It is always fresh, and I think you don't have to buy lemons at all.

That is right. Thanks to God, this tree produces a lot. We squeeze the lemons to make this sweetened juice. Most of the lemon juice is bottled to be used for food.

They all tasted the juice, and Tamim commented:

How delicious, Aunt! Thanks a lot, and God bless your hands.

Fadi added:

That is right. It is delicious. Thank you, Aunt.

Om Wael offering cold juice to her guests by the courtyard fountain

What about that tree over there, uncle Abu Wael? Is it an orange tree?

It is a grafted tree. It bears two kinds of

citrus fruit: one is orange and the other is bitter orange. It is amazing, isn't it?

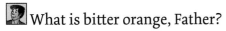 What is bitter orange, Father?

It is like orange in its rind, but its core is squeezed to give sour juice. This juice is sour and somewhat bitter, and it is used as medicine and for food. More importantly, the rind is thick, out of which Aleppian people make a delicious sweet, stuffed with cream and pistachio. They serve it to their guests. As they say, "it is from the bounty of the house."

Walking around Wael's father, they reached the opposite corner of the courtyard. Near the pond, the two boys saw a piece of stone carved in the shape of a conical polygon about one meter (three feet) high. Above it, there was an iron arch, with an attached metal pulley. The arch had two straight sides inserted in the floor of the courtyard around that stone.

Tamim asked:

What is that, Father?

Let Abu Wael tell us about it.

This carved stone here is the crater of the

well. Aleppian people call it "the well's hole neck."

He lifted its cover and lowered a rope with a bucket attached at its end into the well. On top of the well, a pulley started rolling until the bucket hit the surface of the water. After that, Wael's father started pulling the rope upward, and the pulley turned backward. Then, the bucket came from the bottom filled with water, and Wael's father asked this question:

Is anyone thirsty?

No thanks, they said. Tamim's father added:

We just had some lemon juice.

After pouring the water into the pond, Wael's father said:

Now, this way, please.

He walked towards a low opening at the end of the courtyard, which could be accessed by several steps.

What do you think of going down the basement? But watch your head, Abu Tamim.

He went down first, followed by the group.

They went down seven steps and found themselves inside the basement.

Tamim looked up and said, as if he had just discovered something:

 This method of roofing is the same as what we see in many places, in the citadel, the shops in the Medina souks, and other places.

Fadi added:

The ceiling of the pantry basement in my grandmother's house is built in the same way exactly.

Tamim's father explained:

This is the earliest way used in roofing spaces in the past. After that, they used timber beams taken from tree trunks.

Tamim asked:

What kind of trees are used for this, father?

A kind of conifer tree called *al-Tannoub* (fir). Their trunks are tall and straight. Their ends rest on the two opposite walls of the room and carry its ceiling.

Wael's father said:

A courtyard with a pool and a well's hole neck

A basement with masonry vaults ceiling

When we get outside, we will see this in one of the rooms of the ground floor. It is even there in *al-murabbaa* — I mean in the rooms of the first floor. But, look, now this basement is underneath all the

The Rehabilitation
Project of the Old City of Aleppo

This project is a positive initiative regarding the preservation of the Old City of Aleppo. It resulted from an international symposium held in 1983 where the case of Old Aleppo and its conditions were presented. This drew attention to Old Aleppo as an important historical city facing many dangers. In 1986, Aleppo was listed in UNESCO as a world heritage site.

After many communications, and years of discussions, presentations, and dialogue, the features of a newly born project transpired. This project included both preservation of the Old City and development of its residents at the same time. Old Aleppo received two grants, one from the Arab Fund for Economic and Social Development, and the other from the German Agency for Technical Cooperation (GTZ). Thus, the rehabilitation project was born, a pioneering project worldwide. Work commenced in the middle of 1993.

Since its beginning, the project has aimed at involving the inhabitants of Old Aleppo in the development and the preservation process. The idea was to help improve their living conditions in a way that enabled them to meet the demands of modern life. Through this, the goal was to realize a balance between the residential function on one hand, and the commercial and craft careers on the other.

The Old City map was reviewed, and a comprehensive plan of upgrading was laid out. This plan included the

The "Old Aleppo Rehabilitation Project" was housed in a grand mansion previously used as "Saif al-Dawla" school

infrastructure, the traffic, and the provision of financial and technical support to the inhabitants for repairing their houses. Special funds to give interest-free loans were established for that purpose.

The project did a comprehensive survey of the Old City that included urban, economic, and social aspects, and set forth a "building code" for it.

The project set up a comprehensive administrative structure in coordination with various directorates. It included training and upgrading the technical and administrative skills of workers in the project.

Finally, the project encouraged the establishment of developmental projects that are suitable for the Old City.

The Old Aleppo Rehabilitation Project was represented in the Global Exhibition 2000 Expo, held in Hanover City in Germany in the spring of 2000. It was listed as one of the top five most important world projects.

The project also won the Veronica Green Award in 2005, presented by the American Harvard University for worldwide developmental projects.

A permanent exhibition for the project is located in Al-Shaibani School in Al-Jallum Quarter. It was inaugurated in March 2002. It presents the history of Old Aleppo, and explains the process of its rehabilitation. It also presents plans for its future development and rehabilitation. The exhibit features some examples of architectural and building art in the old city. Finally, it includes a 1:500 model of the old city within the walls.

Interior of a room roofed with wooden tree-trunks

rooms of the ground floor, with another opening near *al-liwan*. But here (pointing at an opening which was a few steps lower than the basement floor) this opening leads to a cave. It was filled up a long time ago. It is nearly three meters lower than the basement itself. All I know of it are these stairs, whose lower steps are actually carved into the rock. This is the foundation rock, upon which the buildings of the city lean, here, there, and everywhere.

The group came up from the basement to the courtyard. Tamim and Fadi saw the blue and beautiful sky again. Then Tamim told his father:

Father, I do not know why I feel that this

sky—while looking at it from this courtyard— belongs to the owner of the house and his family.

That is right, Tamim. This is another advantage of old Aleppian houses.

Wael's father added:

While looking from where I am standing, I do not see any distractions of the view. Also, there are no high buildings overlooking and infringing upon the privacy of my house.

He went on to say:

Now, let us go up to the first floor. Tamim and Fadi, listen to this: in the first floor, there are two rooms whose construction I witnessed when I was young. My father helped the professional masons in building them, one after the other. The first room was ready before my eldest brother's marriage. I helped in building the other room before my marriage so I could have it for myself. It is where I got married and lived together with my new family.

Through a stone staircase, with railings made of wrought iron, they climbed up to the first floor and reached the highest point. They stood on the balcony that overlooked the courtyard and led to the rooms that Wael's father had just mentioned. They entered one of these rooms. Wael's father pointed at its ceiling made from timber beams, above which there were flat wood-

A house entry overlooking the courtyard and the staircase leading to the upper floor

Colorful tile flooring inside a room in the house

en plates. In the walls, there were built-in wardrobes. The tiles of the room floor were decorated in a beautiful way.

These tiles are wonderful here, Uncle Abu Wael.

These tiles are made up in special workshops. They are not like the old stone tiling. Each one is designed alone. They are set one next to the other according to a particular design to form this beautiful patterned floor. This type was widely used in many of the old houses.

When did that start?

In the 1920s, they were spread in Aleppo as well as in other cities of the Levant and Egypt. But then they went out of use and were replaced with the "mosaic tiles."

This is like the one in our house, father.

Exactly, Tamim. I think that our house is tiled with this "mosaic tiles." I heard this word from my father.

We also have the same mosaic tiles in our house. I've heard this word from my father.

Before going down to the courtyard, they went back to the balcony, where Tamim looked at the courtyard from where he was standing; from this high point, he saw the pond and the surface of the water inside it, the lemon tree and the other trees of the garden. He also saw the beautiful arch of the iwan. He approached Fadi and started talking to him:

Fadi, look at the courtyard from where we are standing, how beautiful it is!

Fadi paused as if he was talking to himself, but he did not reply. He might have been giving free rein to his imagination, wishing that someone from his family were here with him to see what he was seeing now.

When they went back down to the courtyard, Tamim asked Wael's father a question, as he remembered a word that their host had mentioned before they went up to the first floor:

Uncle Abu Wael, you said that we would go up to "al-murabbaa," so what is that? Why did you refer to a room in the first floor with this name?

At that moment, they walked closer to the iwan, and here Wael's father said:

Let us have a rest and ask Um Wael to

bring us some coffee. It is about time we have it.

No, thank you, Abu Wael. Actually, I have got an appointment right after this visit to your beautiful house. So, we have to go now.

You are not going anywhere before I answer your curious son's question.

Then, he addressed Tamim:

Tamim, you asked about the word *"al-murabbaa."*

Yes, I did, Uncle.

Now if you'll excuse me for a moment.

Wael's father went into the room next to the iwan, which they were in earlier. He walked towards a bookcase, pulled out a neat tome from one of its shelves, and returned to the group. While he was turning over the pages of the tome, Wael's father said:

Look at this, Tamim. It is one of seven volumes called *The Comparative Encyclopedia of Aleppo*. We will search in chapter "M" about the word *"al-murabbaa."*

Wael's father kept turning over the pages

The iron railing of an interior staircase

of the volume until he found the word. He started reading its meaning, while the two boys listened to him. Then Tamim asked his father:

Father, I notice that sometimes you read books similar to this one that Abu Wael is reading. Do you have a similar encyclopedia?

Exactly, your observation is correct. I assume that this encyclopedia is found in most of the houses of Aleppo, or at least, let's say, all intellectual people in Aleppo own a copy. I believe that is necessary for those who want to know more about Aleppo, its people's customs, traditions, folktales, dialect, popular proverbs, sites,

A grand house with pool, staircase to upper floor, and interior kishk

and lots of things related to the City and its people. I think this is a unique encyclopedia of its kind in the world; no city has a similar encyclopedia dedicated solely to it. It is an advantage and hallmark of the city, isn't it, Abu Wael?

Yes, it is. God have mercy on its author's soul. I consider this encyclopedia as my companion, and I always refer to it and consult it.

Who is its author, father?

It is the scholar Khair al-Din al-Asadi. Indeed, he gave Aleppo a present by which he will be remembered after he passed away. But now it is time to go, boys.

Have we seen the whole house, father?

Yes, almost. We did not see all the rooms, but they are not much different from the ones we saw.

Wael's father said:

There is also the roof, where we can see the Citadel of Aleppo.

We will do that at another time, boys. Undoubtedly, you have got a more inclusive idea about the old Aleppian houses now.

You are always welcome, Abu Tamim, and you are welcome at any time, guys.

Thanks, Uncle. God bless your house; it is very beautiful.

Thank you very much, friend. Give my greetings please to Um Wael. Let the two ladies arrange together for your visit to us; we are waiting for that.

I hope that the two boys have enjoyed visiting our house today.

With smiles on their faces, Tamim and Fadi said:

God bless you and your beautiful house. One more thing, please: can I take some photos of your house, Uncle?

Of course, please, and go wherever you want and take the photos that you like.

On their way back home, Tamim commented on the visit, saying:

Father, it's clear that not all of the old Aleppian houses are as big as Abu Wael's house. As we noticed, Fadi's grandmother's is smaller.

That's right, Tamim. Not all of the old Aleppian houses are of the same size: Fadi's grandmother's house is medium-sized. There are also a bit smaller houses with various grades. The bigger houses have bigger courtyards and more rooms and spaces; they may have other different architectural elements. However, what is common among all of these houses is their method construction, the presence of the inner courtyard, and their relationship one to another, whether they be small, medium-sized, or large, in one alley or quarter.

Father, I will write my notes about our visit today, and attach them to the photos that I took of that house. I will show them to you when I finish arranging them.

Good job, Tamim.

Fadi said:

Thanks for having me along. This was quite interesting.

You are welcome, Fadi. Did you like this quarter and that house?

Yes, I did, Uncle. I also liked your friend, Abu Wael. He is friendly and has interesting things to say and appealing explanations, especially when talking about the details of his house. I felt he is happy to live in it.

7

Water Talk

One evening, Tamim came up to his father, who was sitting at his desk, and asked him:

Dad, do you remember our visit to the neighborhood of *Bab Qinnisreen* earlier?

Yes, Tamim, I do.

You told me about the canal that carries water to the houses. You started talking about it when we saw that type of construction inside the walls, in several places, and this is what you called it: *qaem al-qanayeh* (the canal's upright).

Yes, Tamim, I remember that, but what are you trying to say? What is your question?

Dad, since then I've been thinking about an important topic I wanted to ask you about.

I am listening, Tamim. Go on, ask...

I know that water is the cause of life, and

Underground canal dug under a house to transport water

where there is water, there is life. Isn't that true?

This is right, Tamim. Continue.

My question is about water in Aleppo. Where did the water Aleppo drank come from? And what is the story behind the canal that "crawls" underground?

Tamim, I will not take you back to the history books which explain everything about that topic, but I will sum it up like this, so pay attention to me:

…There is no accurate information in the oldest history of Aleppo about water; nonetheless, what is known is that there is a canal called the "Helan Canal." It used to carry water from the springs near the village of Helan (northeast of Aleppo). It was a Roman canal, which started exposed on the surface of the ground, uncovered. Often it was raised on firm structures over low lands on its way to Aleppo, and then it reached the city, to enter through the Canal's Gate or *Bab al-Qanayeh* (which is currently *Bab al-Hadid*). After that, it passed underground through some places, where it had to be dug through the rock, until it reached *Bab al-Arb'een* (near the current location of *Bab al-Nasr*). From there, it branched up inside the City to be distributed into the houses, baths (*hammams*), and other buildings, reaching the church

Two wells carved in the rock to reach underground water, one square (above) and one round (below)

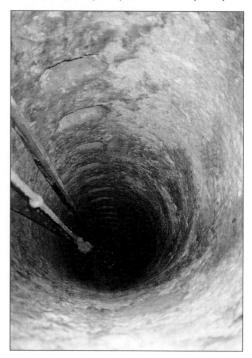

A "well's hole neck" is a masonry carved drum over the well's opening (above) and a photo looking up from inside a well (below)

which was renovated on the orders of *Helana*. This is why the canal was named *Helan*.

Tamim paused for a while, thinking and trying to compare the spelling of both names, then he asked:

Who is this Helana? And what is the church where the canal's water reached?

Helana (Helena) is the mother of the Roman emperor Constantine. As for the church, it is now known as *al-Halawiya* school near the Grand Mosque. We visited it during our tour of the Medina souks and the Grand Mosque in a previous trip.

And what happened to that canal, father?

It fell out of use for a while, until it was renewed during the era of the Caliph Abd el-Malek bin Marwan, who extended it to the Grand Mosque. Later on in the eleventh century, Nour el-Din al-Zanki extended several branches and made it reach the inside of Bab Qinnisreen. After him, al-Zaher Ghazi el-Ayoubi, king of Aleppo, continued to repair the canal, starting from its source and ending in Aleppo. He covered most of it, connected it to the town, extended it, and built pipes along its path. But then the river, along with the springs that supplied and nourished the canal, all dried up. But keep in mind that what was lost of the canal's water because of transportation, evaporation, or leaking, amounted to more than half of its quantity.

I know that today there is no river that runs through Aleppo.

That is true, Tamim, what supplied Aleppo was a river called Qwaik, which flows out from near the Turkish city of Entab (along the Turkish-Syrian border). It was abundant in winter and scarce to the point of dryness in summer. That was until Turkey diverted it to its own lands around the middle of the previous century.

Were Aleppo's residents drinking from that river? And what did they use to do during the summer when the water supply was reduced or dried? And what did they do after the river was cut off?

Originally, that water wasn't suitable for drinking; the river was only for the irrigation of the lands and groves along its banks. Aleppo's residents were forced to carry out a number of plans in order to survive.

What were those plans, father?

Their instincts for survival made them limit their dependence on the canal that provided them with the river's water. So they dug wells in their houses, where they reached the groundwater that existed in the folds of the bedrock. They extracted pure cold water and drank it. On the other hand, they built reservoirs under their houses to collect the rainwater during the winter, in order to be able to drink it and use it during the summer. Don't you remember, Tamim, what we saw during our visit to the old Aleppian house of my friend Abu Wael, where you stood by the opening of the well and asked your questions?

I remember, Dad, but I also remember that I understood from you later, that most of these wells or reservoirs were not used any more. Their water is often polluted, and the issue of collecting rainwater in the reservoirs is not continued and no longer available.

True, Tamim, the Aleppians tried, at different periods of their history, to draw water from the Sajour River, one of the small tributaries of the Furat (Euphrates). But serious obstacles faced them each time, until the government came up with a solution for Aleppo's water in the mid twentieth century. It began to transport the Furat's water to Aleppo in stages.

 And do we drink from the water of the Furat river nowadays?

Yes, Tamim, but that is after it goes through several purifying stages in order for it to be drinkable. Tamim, the water talk of Aleppo takes a long time, and here we have finally reached the result. Aleppo is stable, remains and continues, as long as there is a cause and a chance for living. By this, I think our conversation today has covered your questions.

Yes, it has… thank you, Dad.

—◇※◇—

THE PEOPLE OF ALEPPO

Aleppo's inhabitants are described as a group of religions, races, and communities, all living with each other in harmony. Throughout the centuries, they have been subjected to many calamities and misfortunes, but they persevered, and they always survived the invasions and natural disasters. They were always able to continue and to rebuild.

All the groups of inhabitants from different social strata lived together in their neighborhood, protected by a system of social solidarity that they had developed for their community. They cooperated in handling their quarter's issues and in running its various affairs.

These inhabitants were renowned for their mastery of many handicrafts. They used simple tools, and raw natural material; their goods spread east and west. They used to manufacture and export textiles, as dyed or printed cloth, as well as the laurel soap, made of olive and

Laurel soap blocks drying in factory

laurel oils, which is still desired all around the world. They are also famous for their jewelry and as silversmiths and goldsmiths.

Aleppo's people practiced — and still practice — trading, and excelled in it as well. This was due in part to Aleppo's location as the crossroads of trade between East and West, and as one of the most important stations on the famous Silk Road. But the Aleppian merchants were always honest when they were dealing in the goods that they had received from various sources, or when selling the ones they had manufactured themselves.

Between industry and trade, the people of Aleppo achieved wealth and riches. They were also known for the creativity of their domestic architecture and their skill in its decoration and adornment. The Aleppian stonemason was — and still is — a gifted artisan; he is aware of the artistic value of his occupation. Geometric and floral ornament, drawn and colored, fills the interiors of rooms and large halls, and gives them an air of beauty and luxury.

The people of Aleppo were distinguished by their love for music and singing; they were discriminating listeners and producers of authentic, original, and innovative art. They were proficient in music scales of all kinds, and created the

A house evening concert of traditional music and Aleppian singing

"Qudoud Halabiyya" (Aleppian Measures). They also improved the art of Mouashah (stanzas), and invented the "al-Samah Dance." Their art has become known and valued worldwide.

The Aleppian cuisine has a delicious and special flavor, the hallmark of a refined taste. Arabic confectionery stuffed with Aleppian pistachios is highly prized and has a special place at the pinnacle of this cuisine. The truth about their distinction is summed in this saying: "They make jam out of roses, and make a drink out of almonds."

Finally, the Aleppians are described as good-natured people. They are kind to strangers who are not hostile, welcoming them with cordiality, offering them aid, and often exchanging friendship.

—◇ (8) ◇—
Before the End
Old Aleppo...
the Never-ending Story

Unfinished painting of Old City of Aleppo

Almost a year had passed since Tamim's first visit with his father to the old city of Aleppo. One day they sat in Kamal's office and started chatting.

Dad, you made me love the old city of Aleppo.

The City itself made you fall in love with it, because of its many endearing qualities. In addition to being well built, it is still vibrant after having endured several disasters and dangers. One of the factors that helped its well-being is the tireless work of some residents to halt the damage caused by trying to ram modern streets through it. Tamim, all I did over the past year was to make you get to know it better.

Thank you, Dad, but what are some of those other endearing qualities?

First, it is a masonry-built city; stone can resist time factors, though only to certain limits.

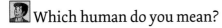 What are those limits, Dad?

For example, a clean environment and a pure atmosphere will help preserve stone, while the opposite causes damage and destruction over time. There are also other destructive factors that mankind is responsible for. The Old City, with its durable masonry construction and unique urban fabric, can last for decades or even hundreds of years, if not damaged by human hands or left neglected. But when this happens, the human role is negative.

Two views of the Citadel entrance towers

Which human do you mean?

You, me, and everyone else. Each from his perspective and point of view. So care is required. Consensus to keep up maintenance and avoid destruction is a pressing issue that needs to be transferred to the next generations — yours and your friend Fadi's, for example — and even to further ones beyond your generation. The Old City is a heritage that makes us proud. We have inherited this from past years and generations, and it should remain for the forthcoming years and centuries. As long as we understand and love this heritage, we will be prepared to protect it and leave it as evidence of the civilization that lived here, on this land.

Is this our generation's goal, Dad? The care, protection, and pride in our heritage, and...

I did not say that exactly. Let's say that it is one of the goals, and there are several goals for your future. Knowledge and hard, honest work give power and result in good things; this also is useful for posterity. It stays as a legacy and heritage that we leave from our present for the future, in order for our grandchildren to be proud of. So pride in ancient glory is not a goal in itself.

You mentioned that the City was well built, and so it remained vibrant. What do you mean by that?

I am convinced, son, that what is good lasts longer. Good may mean more beautiful, or it can mean stronger and better. But in all cases, it reflects its environment and time, and this requires care and maintenance every now and then in order for it to live longer. Do you understand what I mean?

Not exactly.

God bless you, son, I like your honesty. I will give you an example. You know, Tamim, that I like classical music, both Oriental and Western. I listen to it from time to time. So has all the music that has been composed in the past reached us, and do we still listen to it now? No, Tamim. What has reached us from the past is only the good stuff, and that is what we always like to listen to. Because it is nice music, it entertains us and lives within us. It has been written, composed, arranged, and played well; it has its solid rules and still affects us today.

Take another example: the world's museums are filled with rare archaeological pieces and beautiful artistic paintings. Is everything that was painted or sculpted in the past beautiful? No, Tamim. What remains and what has reached us is only the good, so we like it, keep it, and maintain it, and we build museums all around the world for this purpose.

And it is the same with architecture: good architecture that has fulfilled its function properly at some point, and that is solidly and beautifully built, is what remains all over the world. It has also become a pride and heritage for its people, to preserve and take care of.

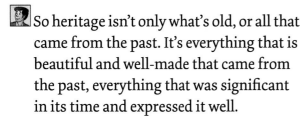So heritage isn't only what's old, or all that came from the past. It's everything that is beautiful and well-made that came from the past, everything that was significant in its time and expressed it well.

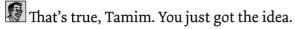That's true, Tamim. You just got the idea.

Once again, thank you, Dad. This subject has become clearer and more understandable for me. Now I understand why this Old City remains steadfast.

Today, the people of Aleppo love their Old City, and that's what's most important. But other people also like this city. Many people around the world are interested in it; in its citadel, its old souks, its neighborhoods, monuments, urban fabric, its houses, and...

When I grow up, Dad, I'm going to specialize in its history, and take care of it.

Tamim, you don't need to make a decision about your future right now. You are today a big fan of Aleppo, and you are excited by your love for it, but leave the matter of specialization for later. You will

Areal view of the Old City of Aleppo with Great Mosque and Souks in foreground and Citadel in background

become more mature. There is no problem with specializing in something else while your love and support for Aleppo continues at the same time.

Dad... I didn't tell you. Along with some of my classmates, and with the supervision of a teacher, I started organizing tours in Old Aleppo at school, like the tours you took me on.

Well done, Tamim. The first step of loving the Old City is visiting it and getting to know it better.

Epilogue

Before the identity is lost, before the insight is blurred, and despite the multiple afflictions today, this City, built with stone, remains.

This silent evidence is a witness. A proud Citadel with its surroundings: architecture and urban fabric, monuments and public buildings, palaces and houses, lanes and alleyways. This is tangible affirmation of previous existence, presenting us with stories still vibrating with life and chanting the spirit of the place.

In the original Arabic version of this book, titled *The Preserved Heritage*, I stressed the need to care for the Old City of Aleppo. I invited its residents and lovers to be good custodians and insure that this UNESCO World Heritage Site would remain as a valuable asset of human culture.

But, alas, events have moved in the opposite direction, and the war in Syria has now entered its fifth year. Hundreds of thousands of Syrians are dead or missing, and many more have been displaced as refugees in the neighboring countries or in their own homeland. Yet, my book still revolves around a preserved heritage. But what preserved heritage remains in a city that is constantly shelled and has lost many of its historical structures and neighborhoods?

Living away from Aleppo, I keep asking myself: Does the Old City still exist, as I knew it? Is its heritage still preserved? Can I still write about a city with the heritage that we all loved, or should I write instead about the martyred city? Or about what we can do to return it to its previous glory? Whatever the answers to these questions may be, I feel that the road out of this catastrophe is long, and maybe

Children of Aleppo drawing the Old City during the "Children and Colors in the Old City of Aleppo" organized by Aleppo Old City Revitalization Project in 2006

I will die before I will ever see my City again as I knew it, and described it in this book.

What a terrible catastrophe has our generation witnessed in our beloved home-town Aleppo. Did history register any agony, grief, and violence in this area like what our generation is suffering now?

The Stone City has time and again preserved itself. Do we destroy what persisted for so long, or do we persist in its restoration, rebuilding, and preservation? So let's think together about how to preserve this heritage, and work to leave behind a heritage of our own to the next generations. Let's shape it with our hands, nurture it with our thoughts, give to it from our soul, supply it with the water of our presence, a presence filled with science and knowledge, brimming with innovation and art.

The City will remain, because it will be a noble expression of our existence and our realities. And since only what's good, wholesome, and authentic will remain, this will be our future legacy.

Khaldoun

Chronological History Chart

Middle East	Date BC	Syria
	8500	Early remains of habitation
	7800	Beginning of agriculture
	7000	Early large human settlements
First World Cultures		
Sumer and Elam	3500	Influence on Syria
Early Kingdoms Period		
	3000	Kingdom of Mari on the Euphrates
	2650	City (kingdom) of Ebla south of Aleppo
Sargon Akkadian Kingdom	2284-2340	
Ancient Syrian Period		
	Circa 2000	Kings of Aleppo identified by names
	1935	Assyrians conquer Mari
	Circa 1900	Assyrians reach Northern Syria
Hammorabi's Ancestors	Starting 1830	
	Circa 1760	Destruction of Mari
	Circa 1750	Hittites conquer Northwest Syria
Hammorabi	1668-1728	
Ancient Hittite Period	Circa 1745	
	Circa 1600	Aleppo under Hittite rule
	Circa 1530	Mitani Kingdom in Northern Syria
Middle Hittite Period	Starting 1500	
Middle Syrian Period	Circa 1500	Egyptians conquer Syria

Historical sequence of political control and important events in the Middle East and Syria

Middle East	Date BC	Syria
Grand Hittite Period	Starting 1430	
	1400	First alphabet in Ugarit
Middle Assyrian Period	Starting 1380	
	Circa 1360	Hittites destroy Mitani & conquer Aleppo
	1285	Qadish battle and division of Syria between the Egyptians and Hittites
Advance of the people of the Sea	Assumed start 2100	
Sumer and Elam	Circa 1200	Ugarit flourishes
New Syrian Period	Starting 1000	Aramaic Kingdoms in Syria
New Assyrian Period	Starting 909	
	Circa 840	Damascus Aramaic kingdom flourishes
	732	Assyrians conquer Damascus and Syria
New Babylonian Kingdom	539-625	
	605	Babylonians control Syria
Persian Achaemenid Kingdom	539-330	
	539	Persian Achaemenids control Syria
Roman Hellenistic Byzantine	330	Alexander the Great conquers Syria
Hellenistic period started by Seleucus Nicator	323	Alexander dies, Syria becomes part of the Seleucid Empire
	Circa 300	Establishment of Peoria Kingdom near old Aleppo
	64	Syria under Roman control
	395 AD	Syria under Byzantine control

Chronological History Chart

Middle East	Date AD	Syria
Islamic Period	632	Muslims conquer Syria
	661	Damascus becomes capital of Umayyad dynasty
	Circa 710	Great Umayyad Mosque of Damascus built
	Circa 715	Great Umayyad Mosque of Aleppo built
	919	Fatimids control Syria
	1097	First Crusade
	1127-1181	Zangids control Damascus and Aleppo
	1146-1173	Sultan Nur al-Din Zangid starts process of defeating Crusaders
	1169-1252	Ayyubid kings control Egypt and Syria
	1169-1193	Saladin fights Crusaders
	1252-1517	Mamluks control Syria
	1260-1277	Sultan Baybars defeats Crusaders
	1516-1918	Ottomans control Syria
	1822	Powerful earthquake hits Aleppo region
French Mandate Period	Starting 1918	French occupy Syrian shores
	1919-1920	League of Nations grants mandate of Syria to France, France occupies Syria
National Period	1946	Independence and French departure

Created in German by Prof. Heinz Gaube, prepared in Arabic by Khaldoun Fansa, translated to English by Mamoun Sakkal

Note on the First Edition

Today, Khaldoun Fansa presents to us the fruit of a heritage literature project. Visit the Old City of Aleppo strives to introduce the younger generation to the knowledge left to us by our Aleppian ancestors in the form of an architectural and cultural heritage.

Khaldoun Fansa is at once a father and grandfather who educates his grandson, through calm and deliberate explanations and interpretations, and passes the assignment of heritage preservation and protection, in a world which threatens us with the loss of our unique identity. All of this is presented in easy language, with simple dialogue, called 'tale,' infused by a humane combination of contemporary and ancient wisdom. And who is more worthy than Khaldoun to take on this challenge? He placed—with charming simplicity—a group of texts, called 'facts,' within the dialogue to introduce brief background information about each site visited in these tours.

From another point of view, the book brings together many of the images published by scholars, before and after the era of photography. Khaldoun has included many rare photographs, selected with care. Several photos were taken by the author himself and are published here for the first time. This book is one of the first to have collected so many images of Aleppo in a single volume.

I am pleased to see the completion of this important and long-awaited project.

Paul Megarbane
Chairman of the Board
Automobile and Touring Club of Syria

My Friend, Khaldoun Fansa

Khaldoun Fansa has stored, deep down in his mind, a strong desire to paint a portrait of the Old City of Aleppo. This city has charmed him, as it has many of its residents and visitors.

With this book, Khaldoun's desire has become reality. Here, he presents enticing details as he skillfully delves into the fabric of the city and examines the ancient threads from which it was woven. His explorations shed a beam of light on the essence of a place that is one of the longest continuously inhabited cities in the world.

The author's experience as an architect enriches his direct and attractive presentation of the facts about the city. He paints a picture of the Old City as a tale of living history. This book is not directed solely to the youth, but also speaks to all those who want to learn more about Aleppo.

Every city in the world has its lovers and admirers, but lovers of Aleppo have an extraordinary bond with it because it has withstood the repeated assaults of history and the acid of time. Aleppo stands as an example of survival. It is a story of endurance.

The current devastation of the eastern parts of the city and the random, if more limited, destruction in other neighborhoods are only the most recent examples. Time and again the existence of Aleppo has been threatened. Yet the tight weave of its fabric protects the city from each blow. With uncanny resilience, Aleppo rises from every disaster and continues on in the march of time.

Walid Ikhlassi
Long-time Aleppo resident, novelist

Afterword

Aleppo! The city that my childhood friends and I were raised in, we loved her faithfully and with excitement, and we hope to pass this faithful love on to our children.

From this perspective, *Visit the Old City of Aleppo* is a book written by my colleague Khaldoun Fansa, who loved Aleppo quietly and wanted to demonstrate, in a simple way, the beauties of the Old City of Aleppo. He does so through a tale grounded in factual texts and pictures, and a lovely dialogue in a question-and-answer format, that enters the minds and the hearts of elders before the youth. With flowing dialogue — like water from a spring on a gently-sloped plain — information is conveyed about buildings and sites seen and felt, which Tamim and his father pass by during their tours, and takes root in the mind of the young boy and his visions for the future.

In the first part of the book, Mr Fansa presents a wonderful glimpse of the Old City, through Tamim's visit to the citadel, the Great Mosque, the Souks and the Khans. In addition, an overview is given of the ancient neighborhood of *Bab Qinnisreen*, *Tellet as-Sawda*, and the permanent exhibition of the Old City.

Then, in the second part, he proceeds to visit of *al-Jdayde* neighborhood, which is located in the northern suburb of the Old City outside the walls, with its traditional houses and churches. He states his opinion on the re-use of some of these houses and confirms the repair of the Old City's infrastructure through the 'Rehabilitation Project.' Later, in one of the visits, he takes the reader to an Aleppian house, and describes –in a simple way- its architectural and environmental characteristics.

When asked by Tamim about the reason for the city's sustainability, Tamim's father answers that "*it is the water*" and continues the conversation about the water in a way that conveys a clear image and a satisfying answer.

Furthermore, the characteristics of the people of Aleppo are summarized in an enjoyable chapter in a way that helped Tamim realize that those people were the ones who built Aleppo and shaped its beauty and charm. With unparalleled creativity, and driven by his love of the beauty of the Old City, Khaldoun — through *Visit the Old City of Aleppo* — was able to demonstrate and affirm the charm and attractiveness of the Old City of Aleppo.

Khaldoun's book is an inspiration to enjoy the uniqueness of the Old City. It is also a direct –but gentle– call to children and youth to protect the Old City and to allow their care and appreciation for the Old City to grow with them.

In addition to liking Dr. Abdalla Asaad's beautiful and expressive illustrations of Tamim and his father throughout their tours around the Old City, I also liked the distinction made in the layout between 'tale' and 'facts' intertwined within the book. Of note as well, are the valuable appendices including the chronological history table of Aleppo and the surrounding areas, along with the credit and reference sources.

The book is an important initiative in educating the children of the community –young and old– and a distinctive approach by which to spread awareness of heritage and the necessity and benefits of preservation.

Congratulations to the Arabic bookshelf. Congratulations to Aleppo by having you, Khaldoun, and having researchers like you. This book makes Arabs, and especially Aleppians, proud.

Abdullah Hadjar
Engineer and Researcher

The City of My Birth

I read with great enjoyment and pleasure the Arabic version of this book, titled *The Preserved Heritage*, written by my colleague, Khaldoun Fansa. Through this book, I have reclaimed many beautiful memories about locations and sites that, until now, I had never realized were such an important part of my life and childhood in the city I left almost forty years ago. Much like a sentimental and nostalgic journey to places that seem both familiar and unfamiliar, I enjoyed becoming acquainted with the valuable information contained in this book about Aleppo, its neighborhoods, and its residents. I longed to visit the locations that were mentioned, but not pictured, in the book. Indeed, I suspect this was the author's intention.

I am involved now in writing about my late father's work as a publisher of children's books in Aleppo during the 1940's, and while reading "The Preserved Heritage", I felt much like a curious child finding answers to old questions that had been hidden in the farthest corners of my memory. I read about the origin of "The Black Hill" (*Tallet as-Sawda*) and its caves, which served as the first population centers in the City of Aleppo. I also delved into the history of "*Al-Jdayde* Quarter," which functioned as a model for peaceful coexistence between different sects and exhibited fraternal tolerance toward all of the City's inhabitants. I felt that the author acted as a conscientious father and a gentle teacher in conveying this information to his readers of all ages.

The story is delightful, the information engaging and edifying, and the presentation beautiful and charming. The author's intimate knowledge of Aleppo, its architecture, and its history is evident throughout the book, but especially in those pages of '*facts*'. Perhaps one of the most important characteristics of *The Preserved Heritage*, however, is the author's focus on the role that Aleppo's inhabitants played in building and preserving their City. In doing so, he addresses a new generation of Aleppians and reminds them of the importance of their heritage and of the responsibility of each individual to maintain and conserve it.

With the support of its board chairman, Paul Megarbane, The Automobile and Tourism Club of Aleppo first published 'Visit the Old City of Aleppo' in Arabic in 2007, under the title 'The Preserved Heritage.' Its translation to English comes at a time when the city is suffering immensely form the ravages of war and destruction. Many of the irreplaceable places lovingly pictured and described in this book lie now in ruins, and without an end in sight, the hearts of all those who lived in and loved Aleppo are filled with sadness, sorrow, and despair. The Epilogue added at the end of the book expresses the sentiments we all feel towards the heritage destruction of the Old City of Aleppo and laments the terrible conditions of ruined sites.

We are grateful to Cune Press for publishing *Visit the Old City of Aleppo* at this crucial time in the City's history. This book is bound to play an important role in reminding us of the value of this World Heritage Site, and in encouraging us to become involved in its rescue, rebuilding, protection, and preservation. The Old City of Aleppo is a beautiful story that should not have a tragic ending during our own lifetime.

Mamoun Sakkal, PhD
Designer and Researcher

Old Dabbagha Mosque, Aleppo
Mamoun Sakkal, 1973

Acknowledgments

Three interesting books written by German authors and intended for their children inspired my writing of this book.

What distinguishes these books is their transmission of ideas through simple illustrations and attractive, accurate information. These publications, and others, have led me to ask, "Shouldn't we be writing for our own children, acquainting them with the story of Old Aleppo from the beginning?"

Mari, a Place Worth Visiting (*Mari, ist eine Reise wert*) From the Mediterranean to the Euphrates – 4,000 years ago. By Helga Strommenger, a children's illustrator.

Helga visited Syria with her sister, Eva Strommenger, an archaeologist working in the large digs at Habuba. Eva introduced Helga to the ancient city of Mari, which was discovered under Tel Hariri, a hill in the al-Jazeera area of Syria. Helga learned details regarding the origin of the local culture and wished to pass these along to the children and youth of Germany. She used illustrations to do this and clarified her information with detailed drawings of each site or incident. Eva wrote the accompanying text, which, although simple and elegant, also clarified and verified the content of the illustrations.

The book was published in 1982 in Mainz, Germany.

Jamil's Guest (*Zu Gast bei Jamil*) by Karin Schmidel

This book is aimed at 6-10 year old children. The illustrations were used to clarify the text's content. It tells the story of the Aleppo room on display in the Museum of Islamic Art in Berlin. The room was originally taken from *Beit Wakeel* in the Jdayde quarter of Old Aleppo. The book also includes information on the history, architecture, arts, crafts, and social life of Aleppo.

All of this is in the form of a true, illustrated story that the Aleppian boy, Jamil, tells his guests.

This has been taken from a publication by the Berlin Museum in 2000.

Balduin and the Mysterious Heritage (*Balduin und das Räselhafte Erbe*) by Karen Ermete, Illustrations by Mesut Eydin.

Published by the Museum of Nature and Humanity, Oldenburg, Germany, 2006, on the occasion of the opening of the "Salah al-Din and the Crusaders" exhibit.

This highly informative book is written for youth and children over age 10. It tells the story of Balduin, a young German boy, who asks about the Levantine cultural fusion that occurred between the Crusaders and the Muslims during the twelfth and thirteenth centuries. Ermete has woven a great deal of historical fact into the fabric of Balduin's story, thus giving a truer picture of the Crusades, the reasons behind them, Salah al-Din, and all facets of the local culture.

*   *   *

Finally, I remembered a book that had been on my shelf for a few years and had captured my attention when I first bought it; I realized that it deserves to be mentioned as a fourth book in this genre.

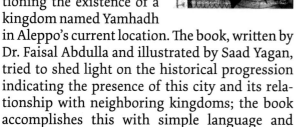

Written in Arabic, the book's title is: **Taj Halab: the Story of the Oldest City on Earth** ("*Taj Halab*" means "Aleppo's Crown"). It tells the story of Aleppo, as reported by tablets from Ebla and Mari mentioning the existence of a kingdom named Yamhadh in Aleppo's current location. The book, written by Dr. Faisal Abdulla and illustrated by Saad Yagan, tried to shed light on the historical progression indicating the presence of this city and its relationship with neighboring kingdoms; the book accomplishes this with simple language and large print, targeting young people who know little about Aleppo's origins.

It was published by architects Hanifa Jabri and Omar Abdul-Aziz al-Hallaj, and printed by Dar el-Elm in Damascus.

*   *   *

Thanks are due to:

The authors, illustrators, and publishers of these four books. They were the instigators of cultural artifacts well worth our gratitude;

The Automobile and Tourism Club of Syria, the publisher of the Arabic version of this book, led and directed by Paul Megarbane.

Dr. Munzer Absi and Mustafa Merza for translating this book into English.

And finally, my special thanks:

To Dr. Mamoun Sakkal for his valuable time and efforts in reviewing, editing and making this English version of the book a dream come true,

To John D. Berry for editing the English text and making it ever more readable, and

To Scott Davis and Cune Press for believing in 'Our Heritage' and publishing my this to the world.

You all have my respect and gratitude.

Khaldoun Fansa

About the References and Resources

I wasn't the first to write about the Old City of Aleppo, nor will I be the last. It was axiomatic for me to refer, as others would, to available historical references that cover most of the subjects presented in this book, both in the Tale and the Facts sections.

Nevertheless, I don't want to provide a bibliography about the history of Aleppo, as others usually do, since many of these references are well known and readily available in many books written about Aleppo. Rather, I will give a brief summary of only the most important reference books I consulted.

I referred to Ibn Shaddad's book, *Al-Aalaq Al-Khateera*, and the Russell Brothers' book *The Natural History of Aleppo* in several sections of this book, like my "Talk of Water." As for the history of the Citadel and description of its structures, I referred to *Kunooz Al-Thahab* by Sabt Ibn Al-Ajami and *Aleppo Citadel* by Faisal Sairafi and Nader Al-Attar. When I was writing about the history of the Citadel and the City, I drew on *Zubdet Al-Halab* by Ibn Al-Adeem, and *Nahr Al Thahab* by Al-Ghazzi among others. For the essay on *Tallet as-Sawda* and the origin of the City, I leaned on an essay written by Khair al-Din al-Asadi, published in 1970, and on his *Comparative Encyclopedia of Aleppo* in other places in the book.

I have to admit that I took the easy route sometimes, and referred to modern books, which in turn were based on previous, older writings; specifically "Historical Monuments of Aleppo" by Abdallah Hadjar; and I referred sometimes to the author himself. I also referred to "Aleppo churches" by Bishop Neophytos Edelby when discussing the subject of the City expansion and the emergence of new neighborhoods.

To all those who wrote about Aleppo's history, old ones and new, sincerely and objectively, I offer my acknowledgment and appreciation; had it not been for what they recorded, much of the city's history would have been lost.

Image Credits

Numbers refer to page where the image appears.

Fansa, Khaldoun: 11, 12 (top), 13 (top), 13 (bottom), 15 (left), 16, 21 (top), 21 (bottom), 22 (left), 22 (bottom right), 25 (right), 33, 36, 39 (top), 39 (top), 40 (bottom), 42, 51 (bottom), 53, 55, 61, 63, 65, 66, 67 (right), 69-75, 77 (top), 77 (bottom), 81 (top), 81 (bottom), 87, 88, 90, 92-98, 104-112, 115-121, 123-128, 130 (top), 135.

Fansa, Dr. Mamoun: 15 (right), 18 (top), 130 (bottom), 132.

© IFAO (Institut Français d'Archéologie Orientale): 18 (bottom), 19, 22 (top), 28 (and detail p. 38).

Courtesy of GDG Exhibits Trust, Washington, DC: 40 (top).

Megarbane, Paul : 14 (drawing by orientalist artist Pascal Coste), 34, 35 (top), 69 (drawing by Girault de Prangey), 76 (drawing by Eugène Flandin), 102, 129 (drawing by Albert Boche ca. 1895).

Minassian, Mihran: 83 (bottom).

© Museum für Islamische Kunst, Staatliche Museen zu Berlin. Photo: Georg Niedermeiser: 89.

Sakkal, Dr. Mamoun: 8, 27, 35 (bottom), 52 (bottom), 78, 79, 83 (top), 100, 101, 118 (bottom), 146.

Yacoubian, Andre : 12 (bottom), 23, 44 (top), 44 (bottom), 45, 46 (top), 46 (middle), 46 (bottom), 49 (top), 49 (bottom), 51 (top), 52 (top), 60, 63 (top), 63 (bottom), 67 (left), 84, 86.

Notes:

Photographs on pages 18 (bottom), 19, and drawing on page 22 (top) are from E. Herzfeld's book Matériaux pour un Corpus Inscriptionum Arabicarum, deuxième partie, Syrie, 1954. Le Caire: Imp. de l'Institut Français d'Archéologie Orientale.

The image on the "Contents" page is a patchwork showing a panoramic view of the Old City of Aleppo with the Citadel in the center. The work is by Aleppian artist Nehmat Badawi. This piece was hanging on the wall of the office of the honorary counsel of Switzerland in Khan Al Wazir, before the destruction of the building in the current war.

The geometric ornaments used as background on chapter opening pages are a modern interpretation, by Mamoun Sakkal, of traditional wood inlay handicrafts of Aleppo.

Khaldoun Fansa

Is a consulting architect, who managed restoration projects in the Old City of Aleppo. He was one of the founders of "the Old City of Aleppo Rehabilitation Project" and was selected by GTZ (German Technical Cooperation Agency) to establish and manage the "Residents Lending Fund" between 1993 and 2001. He was a contributor to the German exhibitions "Damascus – Aleppo: 5000 Years of Civic Development" in 2000, and "Saladin and The Crusaders" in 2006.

Mr Fansa presented and published several papers related to the Old City of Aleppo and worked as a consultant to the Aga Khan Trust for Culture as a manager of the Preservation Work in the Citadel of Aleppo and the Citadel of Masyaf, between 2000 and 2008. He was a founding member of "Aleppo Citadel Friend Society" in 2006.

Abdalla Asaad

Abdalla Asaad is an artist and illustrator with a PhD in Art Criticism. He participated in many art exhibitions locally and internationally. His graphic work includes poster designs for festivals, cartoons for Al-Domari Magazine, and comics for Usama children's magazine and other newspapers in Syria. Mr Asaad was the Plastic Arts Professor at Al-Kalmoun University in central Syria.